FAITH

JOSEPH'S STORY

A Novel and Christian
Bible Study

SANDRA LEA HARDAGE

Hardage Publications
www.sandrahardage.com

ISBN-13:9781514105276
ISBN-10:1514105276

Library of Congress Control Number: 2013908250

Printed in the United States of America.

This book is printed on acid-free paper.

Photo for cover and author page:
Photograph by Viva Rose Photography, 2013.

Dedicated to my family:
Jim, Beth, Jen, Chad, Matt, Carissa, Nathan, Drew,
Jake, Abby Lea, Maggie, Ella, Elijah, and Levi, and
to my ancestors who shared their faith in Jesus Christ.

But Joseph said to them, "Don't be afraid.
Am I in the place of God? You intended to harm me,
but God intended it for good to accomplish what is now being done,
the saving of many lives."
Gen 50:19-20

CONTENTS

PREFACE

While my own life has not been as dramatic and eventful as Joseph's life, the Lord placed on my heart affection for Joseph and a vision of the parallels between our lives.

I came from a family that loved me. I was the oldest of four girls and my family, like other families, passed down both good and bad genetic, spiritual, and environmental attributes to the next generation. Since parents don't receive a set of instructions the day their children are born, they must do their best based on what they know. That is what my parents did.

They taught me a love for Jesus. I have learned through a probe into my own genealogy that the teaching of Christianity does exist in families including my own. It may be passed from one generation to the next, coming down by ancestors far removed. In my family, I can trace a genealogy of faith in Christ to many of my ancestors including a preacher named John Rodgers, who aided William Tyndale in translating the Bible into English and was burned at the stake in 1555 because of his strong beliefs.

I have great-great grandmothers and grandfathers who had their own personal walk with Jesus Christ. It is such a blessing to me to have proof of this through books, letters and family stories. I pray that all my descendants will be able to see physical evidence in something I leave behind, showing my faith in Jesus Christ as my Lord and Savior.

Having a Christian lineage does not mean that your family automatically passes down a love and faith in Jesus Christ from family member to family member. Faith is a personal trait and one that every person must acquire on his own. It is learning how to trust in what God has done and what He will do in your life. Just as in Joseph's life, the faith of Abraham, Isaac, and Jacob did not become Joseph's faith until his life took an unexpected turn.

Knowledge of and belief in God and His promises were the most important traits passed down to Joseph from Abraham, Isaac, and Jacob. But we also see that Joseph's family inherited several bad traits, including favoritism, jealousy, sibling rivalry, plotting, scheming, and deceitfulness.

Thankfully, God does not punish us for our parents' sins, but the effects can still be felt. Our spiritual heritage and lineage can lay the foundation of faith that will overpower and disable the negative effects of our family's physical lineage.

The measure of a person's character is not what is passed down to him from his ancestors but what he leaves his descendants. This is what we see in Joseph. He developed such a strong faith that he recognized that even though the circumstances were bad, God was still in control and had a plan for his life.

Our journey of faith leads us one step at a time toward total assurance and trust in God. When we learn that we can trust God, we can be assured that all things are under His control, in His timing, and according to His plan. Joseph came to rely on God through the adversities and trials he encountered. He matured in his faith through finding assurance in trusting God in all circumstances. Once Joseph reached the place of power in Pharaoh's court, he realized that God had been preparing him all along for the position of vizier and for saving the lives of thousands of people.

In my own journey of faith, I have learned that relying on God day by day and step by step is essential for a maturing trust and faith in Him. Daily experiences soon become life experiences. God prepares you daily to move toward the tasks He has prepared for your life.

As a daughter, wife, mother, grandmother, and teacher, God has been preparing me for the tasks He had planned for this exact time in my life. Most times, God surprises me. It was not my plan to become involved with video production, technology, or distance learning. In fact, when I was in high school, there was no such thing as a personal computer much less the Internet. Yet through the course of my life, my professional career has taken me from classroom teaching to online teaching. It was during this time, I learned basic knowledge and skill of computers, video production, and curriculum development for teaching.

It was not my plan to work in television, but I soon found myself as coordinator of the GED-ONTV program on our state PBS television network. It was here that I learned the inner workings of television production from scriptwriting, videotaping, producing and hosting live on-air broadcasts.

It was not my plan to work on statewide programs using distance learning and technology for classroom use, teaching educators how to use personal computers and technology for instruction, or founding a statewide distance-learning center for delivering curriculum content for high school classrooms via videoconferencing. I learned more about computer software, distance learning, computer networking, the Internet, webpage design and how to use each of these things for the classroom to enhance learning.

It was not my plan to teach God's Word in a Sunday school class or work in women's ministry to encourage women in their Christian walk. It was not my plan to create an online ministry for that purpose or produce video lessons for an online Bible study. It certainly was not my plan to write a book. But somehow, God has brought me to these steps.

I believe God has been training me all my life for the task He has given me today, just as Joseph was being prepared to be vizier of Egypt during a time of plenty and of famine.

As you read the story of Joseph's life, see God's hand in the reasons He brought Joseph to power in Egypt, and then recognize His hand in your own life as He prepares you for tasks He planned for you before you were born.

May God richly bless you in your own journey of faith as you walk one step at a time toward Finding Assurance In Trusting Him also known as FAITH.

ACKNOWLEDGMENTS

To my Christian family at First Baptist Church in Bismarck, Arkansas, who allowed me the privilege to teach lessons on Joseph in face-to-face mode and through the online format of live teleconferencing and videos. And especially to my friends Wanda Berry, Susie Spann, Debbie Sutton and my sister Brenda Magee who helped edit my thoughts and encourage me. I thank you all for the prayers, support, and love you have shown.

INTRODUCTION

In the ancient land of Canaan, Abraham, the grandfather of Jacob, led his family in worship of YHWH, the Almighty Sovereign God and Creator of the universe. YHWH had called Abram to leave his homeland and settle in a land God would show him. Because of his obedience, YHWH would make a covenant with him and change his name to Abraham. This covenant promised eternal possession of the Promised Land, Abraham's descendents would be as numerous as the stars in the sky, and YHWH would take care of them and protect them wherever they would go. Abraham passed the covenant promise to his son, Isaac who then passed it to his son Jacob who passed the promise to following generations.

Residing in the land of Canaan, the tribe of Jacob grew large in number. His people moved from place to place and lived in tents while tending their livestock and seeking green pastures.

Jacob became wealthy and was highly respected by the surrounding tribes. He had many flocks and many sons—twelve to be exact. He had two wives, Leah and Rachel (the wife he loved the most), and two concubines, Bilhah and Zilpah.

Jacob's family had been troubled with deceit, jealousy, lies, and schemes. Jacob deceived his father for the birthright, and Laban, Jacob's uncle, had switched his daughter Rachel for his older daughter Leah at the wedding ceremony, ensuring a sibling rivalry that would affect Jacob's children for years to come.

Rachel and Jacob had wanted a son for many years. Rachel was barren in a patriarchal culture that considered infertility a female defect. Often the barren woman was considered cursed by God and ostracized by other women. But when Rachel's son Joseph was born, Jacob was delighted and showered Joseph with much attention. Joseph was his favorite son. When Rachel died giving birth to her second son, Benjamin, Joseph became the center of Jacob's world.

Because of his favored position with his father, Joseph's many brothers grew so jealous of the attention he received that they began to hate him. They devised a plan that ultimately would rip out their father's heart and start a series of events leading to something the brothers never expected.

This is the story of Joseph. He encountered many trials in his life. He was hated by his brothers and sold into slavery. He was tempted by his master's wife, accused of rape and sent to prison by her angry husband Potiphar. But through it all, Joseph relied on YHYW, the Sovereign God and Creator of the universe.

Joseph's story expresses how faith can carry people through difficult times, even when there seems to be no way out. His faith would mature and grow to the point of understanding God's plan for his life. Listen carefully as Joseph tells his story.

CHAPTER 1

Family Life

Joseph Reveals His Dreams to His Brethren

I am Joseph, vizier and second in command under the great Pharaoh, King of Egypt. I am known by my Egyptian name, Zaphenath-Paneah and nothing happens in this land except through me.

I am very powerful, with the charge of life and death over man and beast. I live in a beautiful palace and have everything I desire—the best this earth has to offer. It has not always been this way, for I was not born to royalty.

My life began in the home of a large wealthy family living in a culture very different from Egypt. My family led an agrarian lifestyle. We moved often to pasture the large numbers of sheep and other livestock we owned. Most of the time, our pastures were located in the rich land of the Hebron Valley in southern Canaan.

My grandfather was Isaac, and my great-grandfather was Abraham. I learned about the living YHWH through my family's great faith, but it would take a series of tragic events for me to develop a personal relationship with YHWH.

You see, long ago, YHWH had promised Abraham that from his seed would come many nations and kings. YHWH also promised that Abraham's descendents would go down to a foreign land and live in exile for four hundred years. They eventually would become slaves before returning to the Promised Land YHWH had given them.

I couldn't help but wonder about my part in this promise and, looking back, I see that YHWH had set a plan in motion that would dramatically change my life and my family's life.

My father was Jacob, or Israel as he eventually would be known, and my mother was Rachel. My father fell deeply in love with my mother the first time he saw her. He had asked her father, Laban (who was also my father's uncle) for her hand in marriage. Since my father did not have the bride price or dowry, Laban had my father work for seven years for my mother's hand in marriage.

But my great-uncle played a terrible trick on my father on his wedding day. My uncle switched my mother for her sister, Leah, and my father unknowingly married Leah instead. He was furious, but he married my mother seven days later after promising to work for Laban for an additional seven years as a dowry. My father now had two wives and eventually ended up with two more wives when my mother and my aunt gave their handmaidens to my father so they could bear children.

There seemed to be great competition between my mother and Aunt Leah as far as bearing children. Aunt Leah would bear many sons, and this made my mother so sad that she had not conceived at all. Soon jealousy took hold, and many arguments followed as the two women tried to satisfy my father and gain his attention.

This might seem strange, but during this time, the number of male children a woman bore defined her and her position in society. My mother was very beautiful, and my father loved her and favored her. This made Aunt Leah feel as if she were not loved at all. She thought the only way she could gain my father's attention was to give him sons. The more children she had, the more my mother envied her sister because my mother was barren. Aunt Leah gave birth to Reuben, Simeon, Levi, Judah, Issachar, and Zebulon.

Soon my mother became desperate for a child and gave her handmaiden, Bilhah, to bear a child for her. Bilhah had two sons by my father, Dan and Naphtali. Aunt Leah had stopped bearing children for a while, so she gave her handmaiden, Zilpah, to my father so they could have children together. Zilpah gave birth to Gad and Asher.

Eventually, my mother became pregnant and I was born. She was so excited, and my father was very proud. He called me the son of his old age. It was evident that my father was more proud of me than his other children.

I looked so much like my mother that my father showered his love and affection on me in many ways. I received the best of everything: the choicest food, the best grazing places for my sheep, the honored position next to my father at meals, the optimal location for my tent, and a place next to my father everywhere he went.

Then my father decided to return home to the land where he was born. My mother was pregnant again and was soon to deliver my brother Benjamin. Then, just as we were near a place that would one day be called Bethlehem, my mother went into labor. Shortly after Benjamin was born, my mother died. My father grieved so much for my mother that I thought perhaps he would die too. Soon my father doted on me to the point that he barely let me out of his sight.

Because he loved me so much, my father had a beautiful coat made just for me—a coat unlike any in my country and certainly one too beautiful to wear while tending sheep. I had heard only royalty had anything to compare to this special coat, which was multicolored and carefully woven. I loved this coat so much I just had to wear it all the time, and I admit that I sometimes gloated about it in my brothers' presence.

This coat was more than just a beautiful garment; it represented my father's intention to give me the birthright. Reuben, my father's oldest son, had forfeited the birthright by having an affair with Bilhah, and Simeon and Levi were passed over for the violent killings they committed in connection with the rape of their sister Dinah. That meant Judah and I were eligible for the birthright. Because of the coat and my father's favoritism toward me, my brothers were certain I would receive my father's birthright.

Having the birthright would put me in an important position: I would receive the inheritance as head of the family. I would make decisions regarding all family matters, offering sacrifices as spiritual leader, and I also would receive a double portion of everything, including all material wealth.

My brothers were extremely jealous and bitter about this, so they sought to eliminate their problem: me. I did not understand the extent of their hatred for me until "that day" when my whole life changed. I now realize that in my youth I was boastful and proud, and as a result I helped provoked my brothers to jealousy.

Part of my brothers' jealousy revolved around a special gift given to me by YHWH. He gave me special dreams and later the ability to interpret the dreams of others. This gift would save thousands of lives, but as a teen, I understood little about YHWH and my attitude was not at all godly. You might even say I was prideful.

When I was seventeen, YHYW gave me two dreams that greatly angered my brothers. God didn't tell me to report these dreams to my brothers, but I was so excited about them that I felt compelled to share.

My brothers were in the pasture one day when I shared my first dream. I found them resting near the flock, so I perched myself on a rock and began telling them what they didn't want to hear. In my first dream, my brothers and I were binding sheaves of grain in the field. My sheaf stood up, and my brothers' sheaves gathered around mine and bowed down to my sheaf.

It was a simple dream, but I didn't realize how angry they would become. Once I told them about this dream, they angrily asked if I thought I was going to reign over them. It really made them mad.

Not long after that, I had a second dream. This time my father and brothers were sitting eating a meal near our tents. The sun, moon, and eleven stars were bowing down to me. My father recognized the meaning of the dream immediately and asked me if he, my brothers, and mother were all going to bow down to me. This dream caused a much stronger reaction than the first. My brothers jumped to their feet and angrily told me I was prideful and arrogant. It took my brothers quite a while to settle down from their anger.

My father also seemed troubled by the dreams. He later shared with me after we were reunited in Egypt that he had kept these dreams to himself discussing them with no one. He wondered how God would bring about this dream prophecy. It was even harder to understand the meaning of the dreams during his many times of overwhelming grief when he thought I was dead. He wondered if God had made a mistake.

I had no idea at this point in my life exactly what these God-given dreams meant or if they would come to pass. Little did I know that many years later my brothers would be brought before me and would bow down before me just as the dreams had predicted.

CHAPTER 2

Sold into Slavery

Jacob Mourns His Son Joseph

My brothers' jealousy grew worse. They became very bitter toward me, so I stayed close to my father as often as I could. This made them all the angrier. If I walked up to them, they would turn from me or make jokes about me and laugh. I thought they would get over their jealousy because we were family, but I was wrong. Instead, everything grew worse.

I didn't know exactly how much my brothers hated me until one day, on my father's orders; I went to check on their progress tending sheep. They had taken the sheep to Shechem, which was a long distance from our tents, in search of good pastureland. I traveled to Shechem but did not find them.

I soon came upon a man who told me that my brothers had moved on to Dothan in search of better pastureland. I walked many more miles to find the field where our sheep were grazing, and then I spotted them.

Perhaps it wasn't the best idea to wear my beautiful coat while searching for my brothers, but it was cold and windy. They saw me in the distance, and the sight of my coat kindled their hatred.

As they spoke to each other, their hatred grew. Soon they devised a plan to kill me and dispose of my body in a nearby pit. Telling my father would be the tricky part, so they decided to tell him an animal had devoured me.

When I got to them, my brothers quickly ripped off my coat and threw me in a nearby cistern that once had been filled with water. The cistern now was dry and the wall too high for anyone to climb. There was no way I could escape unless someone helped me out. I begged for mercy, but they refused to listen.

Reuben hesitated to go along with the plan because he was the one responsible for my safe keeping and the one to explain to my father why I was dead. Reuben persuaded the others to keep me in the pit instead of killing me. His plan was to come back for me later and take me home. Thinking his plan was working, Reuben left to check on the sheep in the nearby field.

After Reuben left, I could hear the others talking and laughing as they sat down to eat. They said such terrible things about me. I never realized how much they hated me. Some of my brothers were still talking about murder. I did not know what would become of me, and I was afraid that I would never again see my father or Benjamin, who was too young to tend sheep and did not take part in my brother's plan.

In the pit, I knew I could not rely on my father to provide protection. I thought the end was near. This was when I realized I really did not know YHWH as my God. I had listened intently as my father told the stories of Abraham and Isaac as well as stories of his own encounters with mighty YHWH. But I did not know Him for myself. Would He leave me there to die? Would He care?

My father, grandfather, and great-grandfather had been through many trials, and God had appeared to each of them. Would He do the same for me? Would He protect me now and keep me from being murdered? What about my dreams? If they had been from God and I was dead, those dreams would never be fulfilled. Was it all my imagination? God had spoken to my father through dreams. Were my dreams real? I didn't understand. I felt terror, loneliness, and depression in the darkness of the pit. I wondered if God was here and cried out to Him to help me.

Then a strange peace overwhelmed me. I felt the presence of God giving me comfort. It was as if His arms were wrapped around me. *Lord God, You are here and You care for me!* I prayed. *I am Your servant. Use me for Your purposes. Use my life as You please and if You choose for my life to be over at this moment, I will be in Your presence with my grandfather and great-grandfather.*

YHWH had made Himself known to me. I had prayed for YHWH's protection and deliverance, and He answered me.

It was there in the pit that the God of Abraham, Isaac, and Jacob became my God and not just the God of my fathers. I was convinced YHWH would provide for me and complete whatever plan He had for my life. I didn't know how He would protect me or when I would get out of the pit, but I had decided to trust Him and allow Him to work through me. I was still afraid, but I knew I now was in His hands.

The conversation that I heard from my brothers suddenly took a different turn. They were discussing a caravan they saw in the distance. Dothan was located near a trade route often used by caravans on the journey to Egypt.

As the caravan approached, my brothers saw that it was an Ishmaelite caravan with many camels and donkeys laden with merchandise. Most caravans were groups of merchants traveling together for safety from thieves and wild animals. This one was no different.

It was a long caravan and included Midianite traders known for dealing in the slave market. Judah had come in from the field and as he watched the coming caravan he had an idea. Judah suggested that instead of killing me, my brothers would better be served by selling me as a slave. He reasoned this would remove the guilt of murder so my blood would not be on their hands. My brothers all readily agreed that would be better, and they also could receive a profit.

So, as the Midianite traders drew near, my brothers pulled me from the pit. I pleaded with them again: "Think of our father. What would happen to him? His heart would break. I am your brother. Why are you doing this? What about my brother Benjamin?"

Again they ignored me and bound my hands behind me. I cried to YHYW for deliverance, but it was not in His plan.

When the Midianites reached a nearby pasture, my brothers went to meet them and made their dirty deal for the price of twenty pieces of silver. I was now a slave.

Slavery was common at that time. Men, women, and children were sold as a result of war and the conquering of tribes and nations. Sometimes people were sold into slavery because of a debt owed or disobedience to a master. But I never thought I would become a slave.

I was terrified. What would become of me? I had lost everything: my family, my favored position, my freedom.

I worried about my father because I knew his heart would break, and he would mourn deeply for me. I wasn't sure what my brothers would tell him. Later I learned they had taken my beautiful coat, sprinkled goat's blood over it, ripped it to shreds, and told my father this was all that was left of me. They suggested that surely an animal must have devoured me. My father grieved for a long time, and my family wondered if he would die.

The conditions while traveling to Egypt were horrible. As a slave, my feet were shackled, and my neck was put in irons. I was forced to walk for thirty days along the trade route to Egypt. No one cared what I said or how I felt.

The only reason for my existence was the price I might bring as a slave. I was no better than the camels. I was property. I asked YHWH what I had done to deserve this and why He had let this happen to me. He didn't give me an answer, but throughout the next thirteen years of my life, He would reveal Himself over and over to me.

I did not know what was ahead, and for the first time in my life, I felt alone. I was totally at the will of my owners. I knew YHWH was with me, but I did not understand that He was using this situation as part of the fulfillment of the dreams He had given me. I did not understand this situation was also part of the promise He had given to Abraham. This experience was part of His divine plan for my life. He had to bring me to this low point to use me for His purposes. He would do this many times in the coming years.

CHAPTER 3

In Potiphar's House

Joseph Sold into Egypt

The first time I saw Egypt, I could not believe my eyes. The land seemed very strange to me. There were many more people living together in the cities, and I understood nothing of their language or ways. I often had heard my family speak of this mighty nation, but I knew little of it and, truthfully, when my father and other tribesmen were talking, as they often did, my mind wandered.

Egypt had become powerful under the leadership of rulers called pharaohs. They each had many highly educated people as advisors and were proficient in government, the arts and sciences, medicine, architecture, agriculture, and accounting methods. They seemed very smart, especially to this Hebrew boy. I was awestruck.

I had heard languages from other tribes when my father was trading, but the Egyptians' language sounded different than any I had ever heard. This highly developed language confused me, but I knew I would have to learn to speak and write it to understand my master's orders. I also would need to understand the Egyptians' ways to survive in their land.

Even their living quarters were different. Looking at the houses throughout the city, it seemed the people were either rich beyond measure or poverty stricken. There were beautiful two- and three-story houses made of mud bricks, unlike the tents of my people. I saw gardens growing in courtyards with servants tending them. Then there were mud huts built for the poor.

The Egyptians' style of dress was different too. They wore scant garments made of linen, and the young children wore no clothes at all. I was amazed to see the women's black hair and what looked like a cone on top of their head. I later discovered they wore a perfumed cone on top of their wigs for a sweet fragrance.

The young men had shaved heads with one braid at the top, and the adult men shaved their heads and sometimes wore wigs—minus the perfumed cone, of course. They also shaved their face, as the only man allowed to wear a beard was Pharaoh, though it was a fake one glued to his face.

The River Nile, which flowed from south to north into a great sea, was along the trade route and seemed to be the major area where crops were grown. I saw many workers harvesting the grain. The Egyptians thought of this river as the river of life.

As the other slaves and I walked to the slave market, I saw strange-looking statues and objects I did not recognize. These were the gods the Egyptians worshiped. My family worshiped YHWH, the one true God, but I soon learned the Egyptians did not know YHWH. Subsequently, I would be faced with many instances where my faith in YHWH would be tested.

Egyptians believed in an afterlife but thought at death the person's life force left the body during the day but returned at night to rest and receive nourishment. Because of this belief, they were extremely careful to preserve the body and provide a peaceful resting place, with the deceased's possessions near the body in order for the life force to rest peacefully at night.

At the slave market, the Midianite trader began to bargain with a man who seemed to be of some importance. His name was Potiphar, and he appeared to be wealthy. As they haggled over a price for me, the slave trader pointed out my youth, good looks, and strength. After much bargaining, they finally agreed on a price. I had been sold to serve Potiphar, so he could do with me as he pleased.

Do you understand how I felt? I had been a happy, free seventeen-year old Hebrew boy just a month before and now an Egyptian was buying me as a slave. I didn't known how this worked into God's plan, but even if I objected, I was no longer in control of my life.

I later learned Potiphar was one of Pharaoh's officers and captain of the guard. He was rich and lived in a three-story house with beautiful gardens and balconies. There was the best of everything: alabaster vases, paintings, hand-woven rugs, golden tableware, golden candlesticks, hand-carved chairs, and even live entertainment at dinner. I had never seen anything like it in my life. But I now was a slave with no life of my own.

As I remembered my father and his teachings, I grew daily in my faith and my walk with YHWH. I served Potiphar to the best of my ability, and I wanted others to see by my actions that YHWH was with me. I successfully completed tasks as they were given to me.

I studied hard and quickly learned to speak, read, and write the Egyptian language. I learned the Egyptian accounting methods and all things concerning the fields and household. I already had experience in taking care of animals and growing some crops but I still had much to learn.

As Potiphar's personal attendant, I took care of all his immediate needs and, in time, I was put in charge of his entire household, his fields, and all that he owned. YHWH blessed me as I served Potiphar, and He blessed Potiphar's house through me. Potiphar recognized that he was blessed because of my God and so he trusted me with everything he had. The only decisions he made were concerning the food he ate.

I enjoyed being in charge of this Egyptian household because it made me feel important. Other people began to compliment me on how handsome I was and what a great job I was doing as head of Potiphar's estate. I dressed in the finest clothing allowed for a slave and had a beautiful coat. Although it was not as beautiful as the one my father had given me, I thought I looked rather splendid. Yes, pride and arrogance returned, and once again the Lord brought me to my knees as His plan for my life continued.

Potiphar's wife began to notice me not as a slave but as a man. She began to flirt with me, and soon she asked me to sleep with her. I knew I could be put to death for sleeping with her, and the Lord clearly does not condone adultery, as it would bring disgrace to both of us.

So I said to her, "My master has put all that he owns under my authority. No one in this house is greater than I am. Because you are Potiphar's wife, you are the only thing he has withheld from me. So how could I do such a great evil and sin against YHWH?"

My comments didn't seem to matter to her because she continued this behavior day after day. Although she was a beautiful woman, I refused her advances day after day because I did not want to sin against YHWH or Potiphar.

One day, when the other household servants were gone, she cornered me in the living area and grabbed my coat as she pulled me toward her sleeping area. "Sleep with me," she said yet again.

All I could think about was getting out of there quickly. I did not want to sin against YHWH or Potiphar. "No!" I shouted. I left the room as fast as I could. In my haste, I left behind my beautiful coat.

When she realized I had left my coat and that I had refused her advances, she was furious. She immediately called all the household servants together and accused me of trying to rape her, showing my coat as proof. Then she patiently waited for Potiphar to come home. When he arrived, she screamed at him, "Why did you bring this Hebrew slave into our house to mock me? Here is his coat as proof that he tried to rape me!"

Potiphar was furious and although he could have had me put to death, I was thrown into prison instead. Because Potiphar worked directly under Pharaoh's authority, I was placed in the king's prison. This meant I was confined in a special prison house under the watchful eye of the warden. In the Egyptian justice system, a person is guilty until proven innocent. Maybe I would be called before Pharaoh; either way I knew I would be in prison for a long time.

Once again, I seemed to be at the bottom of the pit. Prison was not a pleasant place to be. It was dark and the air was stale. The prison was called a round house because it resembled an upside-down bowl. The bottom part was buried in the ground with only a row of open windows around the top to let in some light and air. I easily could have grown depressed and turned my back on YHWH. But even in the dark times I knew He was there.

It was not a coincidence that I ended up in this prison, for the Lord's plan was working all along. Yes, I was horrified because I had been honorable but still was accused. Yes, I was afraid for my future again. I still worried about my father and wondered if I would ever see my family again. But by this time I had learned to rely on YHWH and His promises.

I did not understand how He would use me according to the dreams He had given me. But I discovered that as long as I worshiped Him, prayed, listened for His direction, and confessed my sins, He would not fail me. He already had been faithful to me and brought me through difficult times, and I knew He would do the same now. My growing faith also included knowing that when adversity comes He still is in charge, and I can trust that He has my best in mind according to His plan for my life.

It would take another long period of time and preparation before I was ready for the job God had planned for me. Before the end of my journey, though, I had much to learn.

CHAPTER 4

Prison Life

Joseph Interprets the Dreams While in Prison

There were other prisoners confined with me because they had committed some kind of crime against Pharaoh or a member of the court. Most were prisoners of high rank and some wealth. They were waiting to find out their fate: life in prison or execution.

There is no doubt that the Lord was with me, and He showed great kindness to me by granting me favor with the warden. Because of the job I had done for Potiphar in overseeing his estate, the warden recognized my ability for administration and soon put me in charge of all the prisoners. The warden came to trust my ability to manage and did not interfere with anything that he had assigned me or placed under my authority. Truly, this was YHWH's doing because He made everything I did successful. He was providing on-the-job training in order to perfect me for a special job assignment that was to come.

I learned Egyptian law because I was responsible for making sure all the prisoners, including myself, abided by it. I became well acquainted with the general requirements and characteristics of Pharaoh's court, and I made contacts that would prove valuable in later years. I bartered for food for the prisoners and kept detailed accounts of all the supplies received at the prison. I also kept detailed accounts of every prisoner with a record of when they were sentenced or executed. The lessons I learned in prison were during a time I was most willing to listen to YHWH's leading.

I performed all of my daily duties to the best of my ability. I was learning new things that helped me perform the jobs I was given. I did not know it at the time, but I soon would encounter two prisoners who would change events to come.

As part of my job as overseer of the prison, I was to make daily rounds and check on each prisoner. One day there were two new arrivals: Pharaoh's chief cupbearer and his chief baker. They had offended Pharaoh and were sent to prison for it.

One morning as I made my rounds, I visited the chief cupbearer and the chief baker. They both seemed troubled, so I asked them what was wrong. Each one had had a dream the night before, and they did not know what the dreams meant. I informed them that interpreting dreams belonged to God but still asked them to tell me about the dreams.

Slowly the cupbearer recounted his dream: "There was a vine and on the vine were three branches. Then the branches budded and quickly blossomed. The blossoms produced clusters of grapes that ripened. I took the grapes, squeezed them into Pharaoh's cup. I then placed the cup in Pharaoh's hand."

YHWH immediately helped me interpret the cupbearer's dream: "The three branches are three days. In three days, Pharaoh will restore you to your position. You will put Pharaoh's cup in his hand the way you did when you were his cupbearer. When this happens, please remember me. Mention to Pharaoh that I had been kidnapped from the land of the Hebrews and put in prison even though I am innocent of any wrongdoing."

The cupbearer was pleased with my interpretation and agreed to tell Pharaoh of my situation after he was restored to his position.

When the chief baker saw that the interpretation of the cupbearer's dream turned out to be good, he told me his dream: "There were three baskets of white bread on my head. All sorts of baked goods for Pharaoh were in the top basket, but the birds came and were eating them out to the basket."

Once again, YHWH helped me interpret this dream: "The three baskets are three days. In three days, Pharaoh will hang you on a tree, and then the birds will eat your flesh."

As it happened, Pharaoh's birthday was three days later. He had a large feast prepared for his servants. It was his custom to bring a prisoner to the feast and release him. This time he requested both the chief cupbearer and the chief baker. They quickly were bathed and changed into clean clothing to appear before Pharaoh.

When they appeared, Pharaoh reviewed both men's actions and did exactly as I had predicted: he restored the chief cupbearer to his position, and he hung the chief baker, much to the surprise of the both.

The cupbearer was overjoyed to be out of prison, but he did not remember me as he said he would. Instead, he remained silent and I was forgotten. However, God was working in His own time, not mine. I still had more to learn because I was not yet prepared for what God had in store for me.

CHAPTER 5

Pharaoh's Dreams

Joseph Interprets Pharaoh's Dreams

One night two long years later, Pharaoh had two dreams. He saw himself standing beside the Nile River. He saw seven healthy-looking, well-fed cows coming up from the Nile to graze among the reeds. Next, he saw seven very thin, sickly cows coming up from the Nile to stand beside the healthy cows. Suddenly the sickly cows ate the healthy cows. After they ate the healthy cows, the sickly cows' appearance did not change. At that point, Pharaoh woke up.

But he soon fell asleep again and dreamed again. Seven full and good heads of grain grew on one stalk. Beside these grew another stalk with seven thin and scorched heads of grain. The seven thin heads of grain swallowed up the seven full heads. Pharaoh awoke with a start.

In the morning, Pharaoh was troubled over his dreams and called for the magicians and wise men of Egypt to come and interpret what the dreams meant. These men were those who studied the sacred arts and sciences, read the stars, interpreted dreams, predicted the future, and performed magic. But when Pharaoh told them his dreams, they could not interpret the meaning. Pharaoh was greatly distressed and angry.

It was then that the cupbearer remembered the dreams he and the chief baker had while in prison. He remembered my interpretations of their dreams. He told Pharaoh about what I had done and how I had said God gave the interpretations. He reported to Pharaoh that the dreams had come to pass in three days. When Pharaoh heard this, he immediately sent for me. The guards hurriedly came to retrieve me from the prison.

However, I was filthy and unshaven, so I quickly bathed, shaved, and changed my clothes. Then, accompanied by the guards, I ran to the palace to appear before Pharaoh. I did not know why I was being summoned, but I hoped that perhaps after all this time my innocence would be proven.

As I bowed before Pharaoh, my heart skipped a beat. This man had the power of life and death, and he struck terror in my heart. I had prayed all the way to the palace for YHWH to give me strength to face whatever was to come. I did not know if I would be released or executed. At that moment He gave me peace, and I knew that no matter what was to come, YHWH was with me.

When I arrived, the court was anxiously waiting, and Pharaoh was pacing back and forth. As I bowed before him, Pharaoh stopped, stared at me, and commanded me to stand. He paused for a second then said to me, "It has been said that you can hear a dream and interpret it."

I knew then that the cupbearer finally had remembered me and told Pharaoh about the dream I had interpreted for him. I respectfully addressed Pharaoh and told him that I could not personally interpret dreams but that my God would give Pharaoh the interpretation. He then told me the dreams no one else could interpret.

YHWH revealed the meaning of the dreams to me, and I repeated them to Pharaoh. Both of Pharaoh's dreams meant the same thing: God was telling Pharaoh what He was about to do. The seven good cows and the seven good heads of grain represented seven years of abundance and plenty. The seven thin, sickly cows and the seven worthless, scorched heads of grain represented seven years of famine.

There would be seven years of abundance in the land of Egypt. After these seven years, there would be seven years of famine and the abundance would be gone. The famine would be severe and devastate the land. Because the dream was given twice to Pharaoh, it meant God already had determined the matter and He soon would carry it out.

As YHWH instructed, I told Pharaoh he needed to look for a discerning, wise man and set him over the land of Egypt to deal with the coming famine. He should appoint overseers and take one-fifth of the harvest during the seven years of abundance. This abundant grain during the good years would be stored in the cities under Pharaoh's authority. This food would be reserved for the seven years of famine that was to come.

When I had finished speaking, I waited for Pharaoh's response. I wasn't sure how he would react. Would he believe what the Lord had told me? Would he disregard it and have me executed? I continued to pray that YHWH's hand would be with me. I had peace and the assurance within me that I could trust my God regardless of the situation to come.

I learned over the years of imprisonment and separation from those I loved that my God is always there and I am never alone. I also learned that whatever the circumstances, He was using each experience to teach me. My faith grew stronger each day. He prepared me for large and small tasks, and He gave me opportunities to share my love for Him even in prison. He taught me that when I am in a pit and surrender all to Him, He will give me peace and contentment knowing that the situation is in His hands and not mine. He is always on time with His answers and resolutions to problems.

I knew standing before Pharaoh that YHWH was in control and whatever the next step, it would be God who designed it. It would be part of His divine plan. I can see that what happened next was exactly what the Lord had been preparing for me.

Pharaoh was pleased with the interpretations and asked his servants whether they could find a man who had the spirit of God in him, like me. Then Pharaoh turned to me and said, "There is no one as intelligent and wise as you and because your God had made all this known to you, you will take over my house, and my people will obey your commands. Only Pharaoh will be greater."

Can you believe he placed me in charge of the entire country of Egypt? He removed his signet ring and put it on my finger. He clothed me in fine linen garments and placed a gold chain around my neck. He had me ride in his second chariot and servants called out before me "Make way!" which meant for everyone who heard these words to bow down before me. No one in Egypt could do anything without my permission. Pharaoh changed my name to Zaphenath-paneah and gave me a beautiful wife named Asenath, daughter of Potiphera, priest at On.

It was amazing how my life had changed. There was no way I could have planned this outcome for myself; it had to be YHWH. A Hebrew boy of seventeen put in a pit, sold to Potiphar as a slave, and thrown into prison for a crime he did not commit should have been the last one to be appointed to this high position. But at the age of thirty, I was in a position of power. I prayed YHWH would continue to be with me because, unbeknownst to me, the hardest task was yet to come.

CHAPTER 6

Joseph and His Brothers

The Glory of Joseph

I was now thirty years old. My abilities and my faith had grown along with my knowledge that YHYW is the giver of all things. In one day, I had gone from being a prisoner/slave to being second in command of Egypt. I had been a shepherd, a slave, a convict, and now a ruler. I also learned not to feel too proud of myself because God gives everything—and takes it away.

Remember what happened to me when I seventeen? I had bragged about my coat and how much my father loved me. I was prideful and provoked my brothers to jealousy. I'm not saying I never would have been thrown in that pit because perhaps I would have. I'm just saying that God teaches you the lessons He wants you to learn either the easy way or the hard way; my learning experience just happened to be the hard way. I had so much to learn, and my pride had to be put aside.

As part of my new position, I spent time traveling around Egypt and during the seven years of plenty, the land produced an outstanding harvest. Just as YHWH had instructed, I gathered all the excess food in the land and placed it in storehouses in the cities located nearest the fields. I had accountants stationed at each storehouse to count and record the amount of grain. The harvest was so abundant that I finally decided to stop measuring because there was just too much to measure.

During this time of plentiful harvest, Asenath and I had two beautiful sons. We named our first-born son Manasseh. His name means "causing to forget" and I declared to all that YHWH has made me forget about the difficulties with my brothers. He was such a beautiful baby. I longed for my father to see him. I was so excited about being a father to this precious child that somehow the pain of losing my own father had slightly diminished.

Our second son was just as beautiful and precious. His name was Ephraim, which means, "double fruitfulness". I had been blessed twice with children and I felt so joyful that I declared to everyone that YHWH had made me fruitful in this land where I had been brought by force as a slave and suffered in prison for a crime I did not commit.

Through the birth of my sons, I came to understand my earthly father's love for me as well as the great love YHWH had for me. He had taken care of me throughout my life, and the plan He had devised just for me had now come to be. I was so blessed. I was diligent to teach my wife and children the ways of my people, for one day they would return to the Promised Land.

The abundant harvest ended exactly after seven years. At that point, the crops stopped producing because there was no rain, even during what should have been the rainy season, and famine began.

During the first years of the famine, everyone in Egypt experienced extreme hunger, and the people cried out to Pharaoh for food. Pharaoh sent them to me with instructions to do whatever I said. Because the famine had spread across the whole country, I opened up the storehouses and sold grain to the Egyptians. Eventually even those outside Egypt, came to buy grain, for the famine was severe over all the earth.

I thought often of my family in Canaan. I did not know whether my father was still alive or what had happened to my brothers. I longed to see my father and my brother Benjamin. Had Benjamin grown to be tall? Did he look like me? Were he and my father struggling to find food? Was there enough to feed all of my father's children and grandchildren? Would they survive the famine?

Although I did not know, my father had heard of the plentiful grain in Egypt. He sent ten of my brothers to purchase some. He did not send Benjamin because he was afraid something terrible would happen to this newly beloved son.

One morning, I saw them. They were waiting in the long line to purchase grain from the Egyptian storehouses—my ten brothers who had sought to kill me but instead sold me into slavery.

Though I recognized them immediately, they did not recognize me because I looked like an Egyptian and spoke only the Egyptian language. I treated them as strangers, spoke harshly to them, and did not reveal my true identity.

I asked them where they came from and why they were here. They bowed, as was customary, and responded they had come from Canaan to buy food. As they bowed before me, I suddenly had flashbacks and remembered the dreams I had when I was a young boy. I saw the fulfillment of the first dream God had given me and knew I must not be vengeful, for my God had brought me to this place according to His plan.

I accused them of being spies and coming to see where Egypt might be vulnerable to enemies. They replied that they were not spies but had come to buy food and were all the sons of one man. They claimed to be honest men.

But I again accused them of being spies looking for Egypt's weakness. This time they replied there had been twelve brothers, all the sons of one man in Canaan, and the youngest son was with their father and one son was no longer living. Little did they know, the brother they thought was dead was standing before them.

I was determined to see Benjamin and my father. I accused my ten brothers one more time of being spies and told them the only way to prove they were telling the truth was to send one of them back to Canaan to bring the remaining brother to Egypt to be presented before me. The others would remain together in prison in order for their words to be tested and proven as true. If their words proved to be false, I would know they were spies, and their punishment would be death. I then sent them all to prison for three days.

On the third day, I sent for them. As they bowed before me, I said, "I fear my God and if you do as I instruct you to do, you will live. Leave one of you behind. This brother will be confined in the guardhouse while the rest take grain to your family in order to relieve their hunger. But you must return with the youngest brother so your words will be confirmed."

My brothers did not know I knew their language, so they spoke freely to one another in Hebrew. An interpreter translated my brothers' words as well as mine. My brothers were argumentative and accused each other of being responsible for the situation they were in. They agreed they were being punished for what they had done to me and even though I had pleaded for mercy, they would not listen to my cries but sold me into slavery.

Reuben even said to them, "Why did you not listen to me when I told you not to spill his blood? Because you did not listen, all of us will be held accountable for his blood."

They grieved so greatly about my supposed death that I had to turn away from them lest they would see me weeping.

When I composed myself, I turned around and told the guards to take Simeon from among them. He was bound and taken to prison. I then sent my brothers away. After they were gone, I gave orders to my servants to fill their containers with grain, return each man's money to his sack, and give them provisions for their journey. This order was carried out, and soon my brothers loaded the grain on their donkeys and left.

On the journey home, when they stopped for the first night, one brother opened his sack to feed his donkey. He saw his money near the top of the bag and quickly told the others his money had been returned. They were very afraid. Trembling, they said to each other, "We will be accused of stealing from the great Pharaoh. What is this that YHWH has done to us?"

When they reached Canaan, my brothers told my father all that had happened. They told him the ruler of the land was a harsh man and had accused them of spying, that he had questioned them greatly about their home and family.

Then my brothers told my father the conditions under which they had been allowed to leave Egypt. Simeon was a prisoner, and they were to take food to their families and then return to Egypt with Benjamin to prove that they were who they said they were. Unless they proved this to the man, they would not be able to get Simeon out of prison or trade in Egypt ever again.

As my brothers were emptying their sacks of grain to show my father what they had brought back, out of each man's sack appeared the bag of money they had paid for the grain. They now were extremely afraid.

My father became very angry and said to my brothers, "You have deprived me of my sons. Joseph is gone and Simeon is gone. You want to take Benjamin from me too? Absolutely not! Why is it that everything happens to me?"

Then Reuben said to my father, "Put Benjamin in my care, and I will bring him back to you. If I do not bring him back, you may kill my two sons."

"No! My son will not go down with you," my father cried. "His brother is dead, and he is the only one left. I will surely die if anything happens to him on your journey."

The famine was severe, and it wasn't long before all the grain was gone and the family was hungry. Jacob said to his sons, "Our grain is gone, and we will soon be without food. Go back to Egypt and buy more food."

But Judah said to him, "The man told us as a warning: 'Do not come back to me unless your brother is with you.' We cannot go back without Benjamin or he will not allow us to come before him. Please let Benjamin return with us so we may buy food and not die. If you will not allow Benjamin to return with us, then we will not go."

"Why is it you cause me so much trouble?" Jacob said. "Why did you tell the man that you had another brother? You shouldn't have given him so much information. If you hadn't told him you had a brother, he would not have known."

"The man kept asking about our family. He wanted to know if our father was still alive and whether there were any other brothers," Judah responded. "We had to answer him truthfully. How were we to know that he would say, 'Bring your brother here?' You must send Benjamin with me so that you and all of our children may live and not die. I will be accountable for him. I will bear the guilt if he doesn't return. If you had let us return when we first asked, we already would have already been back home twice by now."

My father was deeply grieved at the thought of Benjamin leaving his presence; Benjamin had been by my father's side for the past thirteen years. My father had to make a decision to save this son or lose the rest of his family to starvation.

CHAPTER 7

Back to Egypt

Joseph Makes Himself Known to His Brethren

My brothers anxiously waited for my father's decision. Would he allow Benjamin to leave his presence so the brothers could travel to Egypt to purchase grain and retrieve Simeon from prison? Or would they be forced to try to survive with the small amount of food they had to feed the many children, grandchildren, and servants that made up Jacob's family?

"If I must let him go, then so be it," Jacob finally said. "May YHWH cause this man to be merciful to you. Also, take with you some of the best products of our land as a gift for the man. Take things not common in Egypt. Put in some balsam and honey, aromatic gum and resin, pistachios and almonds. Return the money that was found in the top of your bags and double it. Perhaps it was a mistake. I pray he will release Simeon and Benjamin to you. If I am deprived of my sons, so be it."

My brothers took the gifts, double the money, and Benjamin and made the return trip to Egypt, not knowing what was to come. They trembled in fear at the thought of what might happen to them as they stood before the mighty vizier of Egypt.

I had posted a servant to watch for their return. When he spotted my brothers at a distance, my servant hurriedly came to me and told me the men from Canaan were returning. I had anxiously awaited their return and wondered whether Benjamin would be with them.

As I eagerly watched and waited, my brothers came into my view, and I silently rejoiced. Finally, I recognized my brother Benjamin. He had become a handsome young man. I so longed to see and hug my brother and my father, and had thought of nothing else over the many months since my brothers had left Egypt. My heart was so full of anticipation, I could hardly breathe.

I quickly told my servant to bring all of them to my house, slaughter an animal, and prepare for the noon meal because these men would dine with me today. My servant did exactly as I had requested and led my brothers to my house.

My brothers were very afraid because they did not know why they were being taken to my house. They were concerned about the money in their sacks. They were afraid there was an evil intent to ambush them, seize them and their donkeys, and make them slaves.

They approached my house with great caution and stood at the doorway, where my servant greeted them. Humbly my brother Reuben said, "Sir, honestly, we really did come down here the first time only to buy food. When we stopped for the journey, each brother found his money in the top of his bag of grain. It was the full amount we each had brought to buy grain. We have brought this money with us plus additional money to buy food. We don't know how our money was placed in the bags."

"May you be well. Don't be afraid," my servant calmly told them. "Your God and the God of your father must have put the treasure in your bags because I received your money."

My brothers were provided water to wash their feet and grain to feed their donkeys. Then my servant commanded the guards to have Simeon brought from the prison to my house to join the others.

My brothers had been told they would eat a meal in my house, so they prepared their gifts for my arrival. As I entered my home, they bowed before me and presented me with the gifts they had brought.

"Is it well with all of you?" I asked them. "How is your elderly father? Is he still alive?"

"Your servant, our father is well. He is still alive." They again bowed down to honor me.

I saw Benjamin bowing with them and said, "Is this your youngest brother? The one you told me about? May my God be gracious to you, my son."

My heart was overcome with emotion at seeing my mother's son, my brother. I knew at any moment I would begin to weep openly. I was not ready to reveal myself, so I quickly excused myself and went into an inner room. I wept profusely. Eventually, I gained my composure, washed my face, and rejoined my brothers. I told the servants to serve the meal and then leave the room.

In the grand dining room of my palace, a table was prepared for my brothers, with assigned seating from the oldest to the youngest. I was seated at my own table, and there were other Egyptians seated at their own table. Egyptians were not allowed to eat with Hebrews because it was considered by Egyptian culture loathsome to sit with a foreigners and shepherds during a meal. They were considered unclean.

My brothers displayed a range of emotions, from fear to astonishment. They were amazed the table seating arrangement was from oldest to youngest and could not understand how the servants could know the birth order. At first, they were on guard, still thinking I might attack them and keep them as slaves. But soon they begin to relax and enjoy the meal. They even began to laugh and talk freely.

They really didn't understand my treatment of them as guests, and all the while they never guessed who I was. I sent food from my table and gave Benjamin five times more than the others. I watched closely to see if there was any animosity toward Benjamin. I did not see any looks of jealousy or hear any remarks that made me think Benjamin might be receiving the same kind treatment my brothers had given me.

My brothers ate and drank to their heart's content as they dined with me. They became more comfortable and seemed to enjoy the moment. It would soon be time for them to leave for home and face the next test.

CHAPTER 8

The Final Test

Joseph Converses with Judah His Brother

It was now time for my brothers to leave for home, but I had one final test for them that would prove their heart and determine whether they had changed, a test that would prove their true feelings toward Benjamin. Had there been any change in their jealous heart, and did they regret what they had done to me?

I instructed my servant to fill each man's bag with as much food as he could carry and put each one's money at the top of his bag. Then I instructed my servant to take my silver cup and put it at the top of Benjamin's bag along with his grain money. My silver cup was a symbol of my authority and to remove it from the palace carried grave consequences, even death. My servant did exactly as he was instructed.

The next morning, my brothers set off on their donkeys toward home. They had not traveled far when I sent my servant to pursue and overtake them. I instructed him to say, "Why have you repaid evil for good? Where is the cup that my master drinks from and uses for divination? What you have done is wrong!"

He set out in pursuit and quickly overtook them. He spoke to them as I had instructed. My brothers were surprised and astonished.

"Why does my lord say these things?" Reuben asked. "Your servants could not possibly do such a thing. We even brought back to you from the land of Canaan the money we found at the top of our bags. How could we steal gold and silver from your master's house? If any of us is found to have it, he must die, and all of us must become my lord's slaves."

"What you have said is proper, but only the one who is found with the cup in his sack will be my slave, and the rest of you will be free to go," my servant replied. So each one quickly lowered his sack to the ground and opened it because they were confident that the silver cup would not be found.

My servant began to search each sack. One by one, beginning with the oldest and ending with the youngest brother, he searched carefully. As he searched through each brother's sack, he found the money that had been placed there. Finally, on searching Benjamin's sack, my silver cup was found at the top of it.

Benjamin was horrified and all the brothers tore their garments as an expression of deep sorrow and grief because they knew what the judgment would be for stealing from the vizier of Egypt. Their thoughts not only turned to themselves and their own well-being but to my father, who was expecting Benjamin to return home. Quickly, my brothers loaded their donkeys and returned to the city and my house.

When they arrived at my house, they fell on the floor before me. "What is this you have done? Did you not know that a man like me has the power to discern the truth?" I asked them.

"What can we say to you, my lord? How can we plead? How can we justify ourselves?" Judah asked. "YHWH has exposed your servant's iniquity. The one in whose possession the cup was found, and all of us will be your slaves."

"I swear that I will not do this," I told Judah. "The man in whose possession the cup was found will be my slave. The rest of you may go in peace to your father."

"Please, sir, let your servant speak personally to my lord," Judah pleaded. "Do not be angry with your servant because you are like Pharaoh."

Judah paused, then explained the situation: "You asked if we had a father or brother, and we answered that we had an elderly father and a younger brother, the child of his old age. The boy's brother is dead. He is the only one of his mother's sons left, and his father loves him. Then you said to your servants, 'Bring him to me so that I can see him.'

But we told you that the boy could not leave his father, for if he were to leave, his father would die. Then you told us, your servants, 'If your younger brother does not come down with you, you will not see me again.' We reported these things to our father, but at first he would not allow his youngest son to come with us. When the grain was gone, he instructed us to come again to buy more food, but we said we could not unless Benjamin came with us. Our father reminded us that his wife had two sons. One left and was torn to pieces by an animal, and he would never be seen again. If we took this one from him and anything happened to him, he will surely die. So please, my lord, because the boy's life is wrapped up with my father's life, if he sees the boy is not with us when we return, he will surely die. I persuaded my father to let the boy come with us by telling him that I would be accountable for him. If I do not return the boy to him, I cannot bear the guilt for sinning against my father. Please let me stay and become your slave in place of the boy. Let him go back with his brothers, for how could I go back to my father without him? I could not bear to see the grief that would overwhelm him."

I could no longer contain my composure. I longed so desperately to see my father. So many years had passed. What would my life have been like if my brothers had not sold me into slavery? I had missed being with my father and brother for so long. The pain in my heart was so great that I had to tell my servants to leave me alone with my brothers.

All the years of loneliness, of being apart from my family, came rushing back to me. All the feelings that I had so long ago put behind me also came rushing forth from my soul, and I could not contain myself. I began to wail, and my weeping was so loud my whole household and the household of Pharaoh heard my cries.

My brothers sat in terror as I wept. When I could finally composed myself, I said to them, "I am Joseph! Is my father still living?"

But my brothers could not answer. They were dumbfounded. They thought I had died in Egypt or, if I had survived, they certainly never thought I would become a ruler over Egypt.

I said again, "I am Joseph, your brother. I am the one you sold into slavery who was brought to Egypt. Don't be worried or angry with yourselves for selling me here because YHWH sent me ahead of you to preserve life. For the famine has been in the land for two years and will be here for another five years without plowing or harvesting the land. God sent me ahead of you to establish you as a remnant in the land and to keep you alive by a great deliverance. Therefore, it was not you who sent me here but YHWH. He has made me a father to Pharaoh, lord of his entire household, and ruler over all the land of Egypt. Return quickly to my father and say to him, 'This is what your son Joseph says: "YHWH has made me lord of all Egypt. Come down to me without delay. You can settle in the land of Goshen and be near me—you, your children and grandchildren, your sheep, cattle, and all you have. There I will sustain you, for there will be five more years of famine. Otherwise, you, your household, and everything you have will become destitute."'"

My brothers still did not answer. They remembered what they had done to me and thought I might have them executed. Perhaps they were not convinced that I was Joseph. I must admit that, at that moment, I did not look like a Hebrew slave.

"Look at my eyes and Benjamin's eyes. Can you not see the resemblance between us?" I finally said. "It is me, Joseph, speaking to you. Tell my father about the glory I have throughout all Egypt and about all that you have seen. Bring my father to me quickly."

I threw my arms around Benjamin and wept, and he wept on my shoulder. I then kissed each of my brothers as I wept. I could not control myself. The tears would not stop. My brothers also felt a range of emotions—fear of what revenge I might take and uncertainty about their future. As they began to see my heart and the joy I felt at revealing myself to them, finally they began to talk to me and answer my questions.

When the news reached Pharaoh's house about my brothers, he and his servants were pleased. Pharaoh said to me, "Joseph, tell your brothers to load their animals and go back to the land of Canaan to get your father and their households and bring them back to me. I will give them the best land, and they can eat from the richness of the land. Tell them to take our wagons for the young children, their wives, and your father to bring them here. They should leave behind their belongings, for the best of all the land of Egypt will be theirs."

I gave my brothers wagons as Pharaoh had commanded and provisions for the journey to Canaan as well as a change of clothes for each of them. I gave Benjamin three hundred pieces of silver and five changes of clothes—much more than I had given the others.

I sent my father ten male donkeys carrying the best products of Egypt plus ten female donkeys carrying grain, food, and provisions for my father for the return journey. I sent my brothers on their way with one last instruction: do not argue on the way home. They seemed to argue all the time, blaming each other for what they had done to me. Clearly, they had not forgiven themselves.

So my brothers traveled to Canaan and when they arrived home, they told my father I was alive. He did not believe them, but when they told him all I had said and saw the wagons that I had sent to transport him to Egypt, he believed and said, "That's enough! My son Joseph is still alive, and I will go to see him before I die."

Jacob quickly gathered all he owned and set out for Beer-sheba to offer sacrifices to YHWH. He wanted to be sure that his God was with him before he moved to Egypt. That night YHWH spoke to my father in a vision. YHWH called him by his name, and my father answered him by saying, "Here I am."

Then YHWH told him who He was: "I am YHWH, the God of your father." Imagine what it would be like to have YHWH call you by your name.

My father told me after he arrived in Egypt that YHWH had instructed him not to be afraid to go to Egypt, for YHWH would make a great nation of my father there. He promised He would go Egypt with my father and would bring him back to Canaan. YHWH even told my father that I would take care of him until he died. What an amazing promise! Was this to be part of the fulfillment of the prophecy given to my great-grandfather Abraham concerning his descendants in a strange land? Would this be the prophecy of the four hundred years?

With YHWH's instructions, Jacob and his family, including children, grandchildren, and everything he owned, left Beer-sheba in the wagons Pharaoh had provided for the journey to Egypt.

My father sent Judah ahead of the caravan to tell me of their arrival in Goshen, where they were instructed to settle. I hitched my horses to my chariot and headed to meet my family there. I was so excited. I had longed for this day for so many years, just to see my father's face, and now it was coming to pass.

I prayed to my YHWH in heaven: "Thank You, dear God, for giving me my heart's longing. How You have blessed me! I had no idea on that day so many years ago, the day I was thrown into that pit, what You had in store for me. Through those terrible times, I knew You were with me. I knew You had a plan for me because You had told me so through my dreams and through the still small voice I heard within me, but I never dreamed that this would be so grand. You prepared me through all these years for the job You had for me for the saving of lives, even bringing of my family to this place. And my brothers—oh, dear God, my brothers! I know that You were using them, and I know their hearts have changed. I saw Judah's sorrow when he thought Benjamin would have to remain in Egypt while the others went back to Canaan. I saw his heart and the heart of the others when they were more concerned over my father's health than they were for their own well-being. My heart has forgiven them just as You have forgiven me for my sins. Help me to make it right with them and restore the years that the locust has taken from us."

When I saw my father, he and all the others bowed before me because of my position. I rushed to him and lifted him up. I threw my arms around him and wept. I never thought I would see his face again. What joy that was! The years had weathered his face, but the eyes were the same. How sweet was our reunion! All we could do was hug each other tightly and cry.

Finally, my father said, "I have seen your face, and I know that you are alive. At last, I can die." He wept uncontrollably. He had thought I was dead all those years and had grieved for me, even to the day my brothers told him I was alive.

After I brought my family to live in Egypt, the famine lasted another five years and ended at the appointed time. My family settled in the land of Goshen as instructed by Pharaoh. This was a place separate from the Egyptians, who detested shepherds and refused to be near the unclean. My family prospered in the land and grew large in number. My father lived another seventeen years, and the Lord blessed us by giving us these years to be together. They were joyful years.

CHAPTER 9

Blessings and Forgiveness

Joseph and His Brethren Welcomed by Pharaoh

My father was one hundred thirty years old when he moved his family to Egypt. There were seventy in all, including Manasseh and Ephraim, my sons who were born in Egypt. My father's family prospered and grew large in number while living in Goshen.

He lived there for seventeen years but grew weaker because of his old age. His time for death was growing near, so he called me to his side and made me swear an oath to return his body to Canaan for burial in the cave at Machpela. It would soon be time for the blessings.

In my day, when the patriarch pronounced the blessing on his sons, it represented a word from YHWH. It was prophetic and had the power to produce the intended results. As was the custom, the oldest son normally received the major blessing along with the birthright. The blessing made the birthright binding, and it could not be taken away and given to another.

Before he died, my father called me to his bedside to bless my sons and to bless me. Manasseh and Ephraim were called to come close to his bedside. I then placed Manasseh at my father's right hand, since he was the oldest, and Ephraim at his left hand because he was the youngest.

It was customary to bless the oldest son giving him the richer blessing while the right hand was placed on his head. To my surprise, my father crossed his arms and placed his right hand on Ephraim's head and his left hand on Manasseh's head. I thought it was a mistake. Father was old and perhaps he thought Ephraim was the oldest son. I started to correct him, but my father refused and told me he meant it to be this way. He gave the blessing to my sons, the youngest one first.

My father adopted my sons as his own and gave them equal status and the same rights as my brothers. He then asked YHWH to bless them. Ephraim would become greater than his brother, and his offspring would become a large nation. Manasseh also would become a great tribe.

Then my father gave me a blessing over and above what he would give my brothers. He told me I would have the mountain slope that he captured from the Amorites in battle as an inheritance. He told me that YHWH would be with me and bring me back to the land of our fathers. That meant someday I would return home. I believed this prophecy. I knew that we all would return someday to Canaan, and I wanted to be part of the fulfillment of that prophecy.

Before my sons and I left my father's presence, he made me swear again to take his body back to Canaan when he died. I didn't know how soon that would be, but since he was so frail, I knew it would not be long.

A little later, my father called for all his sons to come to his bedside. He wanted us to gather around his bed so he could tell us what would happen to us in the days to come. He was very weak, but he managed to give each of his twelve sons a blessing, beginning with Reuben, the oldest, and ending with Benjamin, the youngest.

The birthright did not go to Reuben, who had committed adultery with Bilhah, or to Simeon or Levi, who had committed murder. I was given the right of the firstborn and a double portion of land that went to my sons.

My father's words were prophetic. Judah would receive the promise of a dynasty of kings. Father pronounced that neither the scepter nor the ruler's staff would pass from Judah's line until Shiloh (Messiah) would come. It would be one of Judah's ancestors who would begin the lineage of kings. His name would be called David, and his lineage would end with an eternal king named Jesus.

My father continued to give blessings to each son. He then gave us instructions to bury him in the cave in Machpela, near Mamre, that Abraham had bought from Ephron the Hittite and where Abraham, Sarah, Isaac, Rebekah, and Leah were buried. Then he died at the age of 147.

My heart breaking, I leaned over his body, kissed him, and wept. The time I had with my father seemed so short, and now he was gone. I had his body embalmed according to the Egyptian custom, which took forty days. My family mourned for him for seventy days.

After the mourning period was over, Pharaoh permitted me to take my father home for burial according to my oath. The procession leaving Egypt included all Pharaoh's servants, all the elders of his household and the land, and all my household servants and those of my brothers' and my father's household. The only ones who were not included in the procession were the children. There was much wailing and sadness in honor of my father.

Before we crossed the Jordan River, the procession stopped at the threshing floor of Atad. For such a large procession to enter into Canaan, the local tribes might think that we were entering to make war and conquer them. So we stopped there for seven days. We used this time to reassure the locals of our true intentions and pasture the animals.

This was the first time I had returned to Canaan. I felt such grief and pain for the years that had been lost with my father that once again I mourned for him for seven days with great lamenting and weeping. I also stopped to remember the great times we had enjoyed together over the last seventeen years. I praised YHWH for my father's life.

From Atad, the procession headed to the cave in Machpela that Abraham had bought from Ephron the Hittite, which was my ancestors' burial place. My family buried my father according to his instructions in the cave with Abraham, Sarah, Isaac, Rebekah and Leah. We then returned to Egypt.

After my father died, my brothers were worried about what would happen to them. Perhaps they thought I would have them put to death, that I had been waiting for my father to die to take my revenge on them.

After we had buried my father in Canaan, my brothers sent a messenger to me. On their behalf, he said, "This is what your brothers have said to you: 'Our father Jacob instructed us to say this to Joseph: "Please forgive your brothers from their transgression and their sin—forgive them for the wrong they caused you." Therefore, Joseph, please forgive the transgression of the servants of the God of your father.'"

My heart broke and I wept. I thought my brothers understood that I had forgiven them. I knew in my heart that I indeed had forgiven them, but they must have been consumed with guilt and fear all these years. Perhaps they couldn't forgive themselves for what they had done.

They came to me and bowed down at my feet and said, "We are your slaves."

I said to them, "Don't be afraid. Am I in the place of YHWH? He is the one who holds my destiny. What you planned as evil against me, YHWH used for good. He brought me to this place for this present time for the survival of many people. He knew the plan for my life, and He had many things to teach me before this time. Please, don't be afraid. I will take care of you and your little ones."

As time went on, my brothers came to understand the meaning of forgiveness. The sin that had dwelt in each brother's heart would require a personal encounter with YHWH. I could offer forgiveness, but unless they made it right with the God who created them, all the jealousy, bitterness, guilt, and pain would remain within them the rest of their lives.

Many things in our lives often seem insignificant or trivial, but I have learned that everything that happens provides a building block for the next step. God allowed my brothers to act the way they did, and He used their actions for my good, which turned out for their own good as well.

YHWH knew the plan He had for my life. He knew that I would one day be second in command of Egypt. He knew I would save the lives of many people. He is the one who gave me the gift of interpreting dreams and of administration. I had much to learn along the way, but in every step the things I learned enabled me to perform at my best, based on the way I responded to Him in each situation.

You see, YHWH gives us free will. We can do things the easy way and learn those lessons at the moment He teaches them or we can do things our way and learn through hard life experiences.

Pride and arrogance often get in the way of obedience to God. But rest assured, He will get our attention. He will bring us to a pit where we must realize that we are not in control of anything. He brings us to that place where we recognize that God knows best and whatever lesson He has for us to learn, we must be open to receive.

EPILOGUE

In looking back over the years, I realized I had many learning experiences in my walk with YHWH. Some of my life lessons were easy, but others were not. Either way, YHWH has led me to where I am today, and He has blessed me richly. Here are a few of the lessons I learned. Perhaps these may help you as well.

- **Finding assurance in trusting Him, no matter the circumstances.** This is the basis of faith. If you aren't put into situations where you can grow, how can your faith be strengthened? Learn to trust Him in everything.

- **All things work together for good for those who love the Lord and are called according to His purpose.** I had been called to a great task. YHWH provided everything in His timing. Had I been placed in such a high position too soon, I would not have been prepared. I would have failed miserably and would have caused the deaths of many people. All things happen for a reason. Look for what He is trying to tell you.

- **Satan meant it for evil, but God used it for good.** Satan tried to destroy me because I trusted God and might one day be used by God in a mighty way. Satan hoped that when things got tough, I would crumble and deny my God. Instead, when I put YHWH in charge of my circumstances, I allowed Him to work in my life. My faith and closeness to Him grew. I believed what He was telling me, and I tried not to depart from Him.

- **Adversity creates the opportunity to grow in faith.** My faith at age seventeen was not strong. I was prideful and arrogant as my father's favorite child and in my high position within my family. I knew my father and grandfather's faith was strong but mine was not. Because I had everything I wanted, I couldn't hear YHWH's voice because my own voice and desires were so loud. When adversity comes, you cannot rely on your parents' or grandparents' faith. That is when you come to know in what and whom you believe.

- **God uses every circumstance in your life to mature your faith for a task or purpose He has for you.** He prepares you for accomplishing His plan by giving you "on-the-job training." The years I spent working in Potiphar's house taught me many things about the culture of Egypt and the workings of a large estate. I learned the language and the accounting methods the Egyptians used in trade. I learned much that helped me to make wise decisions in later years as vizier.

When in prison, I did not know what would happen. I had been falsely accused of a crime, and I did not know if I would be executed like the chief baker. But that was not what YHWH intended. I learned from my experience in prison about Pharaoh's court and the laws of the land. This enabled me to perform my duties during the years of plenty and the years of famine in a way I never would have been able to do had I not gained that knowledge. As a result, many lives were saved from starvation, Egypt prospered, and my family grew to be large in number.

- **Forgiveness starts in your own heart.** Don't expect forgiveness to come from someone else first. Seek God's forgiveness for your own sins, and as He forgives you so you should forgive those who have sinned against you. My brothers did a great injustice to me but if I had not forgiven them, I would have been bitter all my life. I would not have been open to YHWH's leading but more focused on revenge. Let YHWH take care of revenge. Show mercy and kindness to all.

- **Use the gifts the Lord has given you for His pleasure.** His gifts are to be used for the pleasure of His kingdom. When my first dreams came, I had no idea how YHWH would use me to fulfill His plan. This gift of interpreting dreams saved many nations from famine. He gave me prophetic dreams as a way to prepare for famine and fulfill my destiny. He gives each of us a spiritual gift that we are to use for His glory.

We may not see the effects of our faith, but we can be sure God will honor our faithfulness. We can be assured that trusting in Him will result in blessings. So as you travel through life, keep your eyes focused on the One who created you. He designed you in a special way for His kingdom's purpose. He gave you your personality and a heart capable of knowing and loving Him. He created you with special gifts and talents for the sole purpose of doing His kingdom work. Love Him and trust Him. Find assurance in trusting Him, for He knows the plan.

When Joseph died in Egypt at the age of 110, he was embalmed and his body returned to Canaan four hundred years later when the children of Israel left Egypt in the exodus under the leadership of Moses. His bones now rest in Shecham in the Promised Land.

BECOMING A CHRISTIAN

1. **Admit to God that you are a sinner and need a savior.** Recognize that you are sinful and sorry for the sins you have committed. This means you need to repent and turn from your wicked ways. "For all have sinned and fall short of the glory of God" (Rom. 3:23). "Repent, then, and turn to God, so that your sins may be wiped out, that times of refreshing may come from the Lord" (Acts 3:19).

2. **Believe that Jesus Christ is the Son of God.** Believe that He died on a cross for your sins, becoming the sacrifice for you; rose from the dead in His resurrected body; was seen by many; and is coming again to gather His own. "For the wages of sin is death, but the gift of God is eternal life in Christ Jesus our Lord" (Rom. 6:23). "For God was pleased to have all his fullness dwell in him, and through him to reconcile to himself all things, whether things on earth or things in heaven, by making peace through his blood, shed on the cross" (Col. 1:19-20).

3. **Confess your faith in Jesus as your Savior and Lord.** He is the resurrected Lord, and only through Him will you be saved. "For God so loved the world that he gave his one and only Son, that whoever believes in him shall not perish but have eternal life" (John 3:16). "Jesus answered, 'I am the way and the truth and the life. No one comes to the Father except through me'" (John 14:6 NIV).

"But God demonstrates his own love for us in this: While we were still sinners, Christ died for us" (Rom. 5:8).

4. **Pray the sinner's prayer:** "Dear Father, I am a sinner and I cannot save myself. I want to turn from my wicked ways and turn to You for forgiveness. I know I am sinful, and I am truly sorry for my sins. Please forgive me for every sin I have committed. I need a savior. I believe Jesus Christ is my Lord and Savior, shed His blood, and died on the cross for all my sins. I believe He rose from the dead and is alive now. I believe He will come again to gather His own. I believe Jesus is my Lord and my Savior, and I will have eternal life in His presence. Come into my heart, Lord Jesus, to become my Savior and the Lord of my life. In Jesus' name, amen."

"That if you confess with your mouth 'Jesus is Lord,' and believe in your heart that God raised him from the dead, you will be saved. For it is with your heart that you believe and are justified, and it is with your mouth that you confess and are saved . . . for everyone who calls on the name of the Lord will be saved" (Rom. 10:9-10, 13).

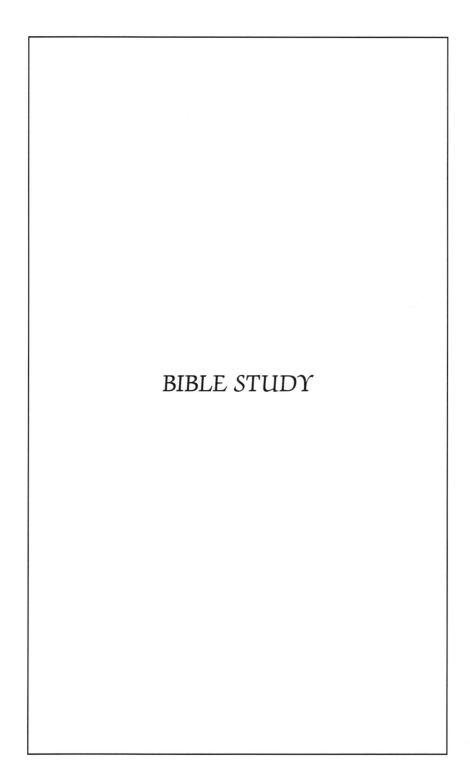

BIBLE STUDY

To understand Joseph's family dynamics requires a quick look back at family traits passed down from Abraham, Isaac, and Jacob. We can pass down numerous kinds of traits to the subsequent generations of our family, whether they are genetic, environmental, or something else. Read the Scripture passages mentioned in each section below, and use them as a guide for discussion and an opportunity to dig deeper into God's Word.

Ancestors

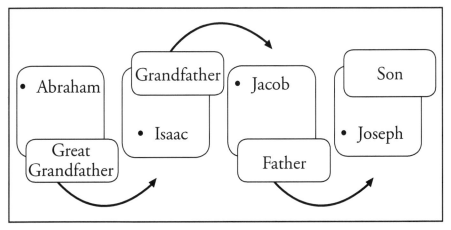

Ancestors of Joseph

Abraham

Joseph descended from a faithful but imperfect family. His great-grandfather was Abraham, who talked to God and was promised that God would make him the father of nations (Genesis 12:1-3).

Abraham journeyed with his family at God's instruction from Ur, an urban city in Mesopotamia, to Haran and then to Canaan, the

Promised Land. God had promised this land to Abraham and his descendents.

While Abraham and his wife, Sarah, exhibited great faith in God, they also experienced doubt in the fulfillment of the promise of a child who would carry on the family lineage and result in Abraham's descendents being as numerous as the stars in the sky.

According to the custom of the time, an infertile primary wife could give her maidservant to her husband for the purpose of producing an heir. If the wife then produced a son, the servant son was displaced as heir.

God did not intend for Sarah to give Hagar, her maidservant, to Abraham. Sarah tried to circumvent God's plan by "helping" Him, and Abraham had a son named Ishmael by Hagar. Abraham's promised son, Isaac, grandfather of Joseph, was born when Abraham was one hundred years old and Sarah was ninety years old, proving that God's promises will be fulfilled in God's timing and according to His plan.

Read Genesis 16:1-16 and Genesis 21:1-21

Because of what had occurred, jealousy and resentment issues arose between Sarah and Hagar that affected peace in this family unit. Repercussions can still be felt today between the Jewish descendents of Isaac and the Arab descendents of Ishmael. There is constant tension between the two cultures often affecting peace in the Middle East.

1. What were Sarah's reasons for deciding to give Hagar to Abraham as a way to fulfill God's promise to produce a child? (Genesis 16:1-4)

2. Describe Hagar's attitude toward Sarah before Ishmael's birth.

3. What request did Sarah make of Abraham? (Genesis 16:5-6)

4. How was Hagar treated by Sarah and what did she do? (Genesis 16:4-6)

5. In what way did God bless Hagar? (Genesis 16:9-16)

6. Why was the birth of Isaac considered miraculous? (Genesis 21:1-7)

7. After the birth of Isaac, what happened to Hagar and Ishmael? (Genesis 21:8-21)

Isaac

Read Genesis 24:1-67

Isaac was the son God had promised Abraham and Sarah. When it came time for Isaac to marry, Abraham sent a servant to his brother's people in the town of Nahor to find a wife for Isaac. The servant found Rebekah who had a brother named Laban. Isaac married Rebekah when Isaac was forty years old.

Twenty years later, Rebekah and Isaac had twin sons named Jacob and Esau. In Genesis 25:21-26, we learn that Rebekah did not have an easy pregnancy and asked God why she was having so much trouble. God told Rebekah that the two sons in her womb would become two nations, with the older son serving the younger.

Read Genesis 25:19-34

Esau, the oldest and Jacob the youngest were victims of favoritism by their parents. Pitting the two brothers against each other, sibling rivalry reared its ugly head between them. Esau was the firstborn child and the one to receive the birthright and major inheritance including most of the wealth, the covenant promise given to Abraham and the leadership position within the family. Esau, however, sells his birthright to Jacob and Jacob received the right of the first-born.

Since Isaac could not undo Esau's loss of the birthright, he decided to give the blessing to Esau and instructed him on what he should do before the blessing was given. Rebekah overheard Isaac's plan and, knowing the promise God had made to her, decided to "help" God by devising a plan of her own for stealing the blessing from Esau.

1. Which son was Isaac's favorite and why? (Genesis 25:27-34)

2. Which son did Rebekah favor and why? (Genesis 25:27-34)

3. Why would Esau sell his birthright for a bowl of stew?

Read Genesis 27:1-46

Although Jacob had received the birthright by purchasing it from Esau for a bowl of stew, the blessing was also important. Blessings and curses were thought to have great power because they came directly from God. Rebekah and Jacob wanted to make sure Jacob received this blessing from God because it also came with the covenant promise given to Abraham.

4. What blessing did Jacob receive from Isaac? (Genesis 27:28-29)

5. How did Esau react when he found out Isaac had blessed the wrong son? How did he express this emotion?

6. As you observe the lives of the twins Esau and Jacob, what type of problems did the two experience in their relationship with each other due to favoritism?

7. What type of relationship problems did Isaac and Rebekah experience due to favoritism?

Read Genesis 27:46-28:1-5

Rebekah and Jacob conspired and deceived the elderly Isaac. To escape from Esau, who planned to kill Jacob after Isaac's death, Jacob was sent to find a wife among Rebekah's people.

Rebekah died before Jacob returned with his family from Haran. In spite of all the deception and hopes for her son Jacob, she never saw her favorite son again. Had Rebekah allowed God to handle the situation instead of "helping" Him, perhaps Rebekah could have spent her last days with Jacob's children sitting on her lap and cradled in her arms.

Jacob

After the blessing and the birthright incident, Jacob was sent to his Uncle Laban to find a wife. On his way, he falls asleep at Bethel and has an encounter with God in a dream recorded in Genesis 28:10-21. Jacob begins his walk with God.

Read Genesis 29: 1-30

Once he reached Paddan Aram, he met a girl fetching water for the flocks. He immediately fell in love with Laban's beautiful daughter Rachel and the feeling was mutual. Jacob ask her father for her hand in marriage and bargained with Laban over the dowry.

The fathers of the bride and the groom usually arranged a marriage but since Jacob had neither a father that was present or money to pay, Jacob negotiated his own bride price with Laban. As a condition of the dowry set by Jacob and Laban, Jacob agreed to work for his uncle Laban for seven years in order to wed Rachel (later the mother of Joseph). But on the day of the wedding, a deceitful Laban replaced Rachel as Jacob's bride with her sister Leah. An angry Jacob agreed to pay the additional bride price for his beloved Rachel with another seven years of labor.

Read Genesis 29:31-35

Because of Jacob's great love for Rachel, he showed partiality to her over Leah.

The sisters constantly competed for Jacob's favor. Sibling rivalry grew strong. Genesis 29:31 states that Leah was unloved, but the Lord opened her womb and she conceived. Leah knowing her sister Rachel was barren and had been for many years, continued to have children in hopes of gaining her husband's favor.

Burdened by a deep desire to have a child, Rachel gave Jacob her maidservant Bilhah to have children in her name. Leah stopped bearing children for a season and followed Rachel's example by providing Jacob her maidservant Zilpah in order to produce children in her name. Envy and jealousy plagued this family, and as a result, the entire family environment developed into one of jealousy, hatred, and bitterness that would cause a chain of events in an amazing story of God's plan for Joseph's life.

Historical Note: Archaeologists between 1925-1933 found the Nuzi Tablets containing cultural evidence and customs of life in the Mesopotamian area ca. 1450-1350 BC. One such contract noted in the tablets was a marriage contract. The contract was between the fathers of the bride and the groom; the bride price was paid by her father to be held in trust for the bride should she be widowed or abandoned. The bride's consent to the marriage was not necessary. The bride was given a maidservant, whose name also appeared in the contract.

1. Why did Jacob travel to Paddan Aram? (Genesis 28:1-2)

2. Where did Jacob first meet Rachel? (Genesis 29:1-9)

3. What was Rachel's occupation? (Genesis 29)

4. What was the relationship between Rebekah and Laban? (Genesis 29:13)

5. Laban had two daughters, _____, whose name means "cow," and _____, whose name means "ewe." _____ was the eldest daughter. _____ had delicate or weak eyes, while _____ was beautiful in form and appearance. (Genesis 29:15-17)

6. Jacob agreed to serve his uncle for seven years for Rachel's hand in marriage and the time seemed only a few days because Jacob _____ Rachel. (Genesis 29:18-19)

7. What happened that caused Jacob to work another seven years for Rachel's hand? (Genesis 29:21-25)

8. Jacob _____ Rachel more than Leah. (Genesis 29:30)

Sibling rivalry can exist in any family. Many times parents unknowingly have favorites and show partiality.

9. What might be a sign of favoritism that you have observed in some families? If so, why do you think it exists?

10. From your Bible copy the following verses:

Proverbs 14:29

_____

_____

Proverbs 20:3

_____

_____

James 1:19-21

_____

_____

James 4:11-12

_____

_____

Ecclesiastes 7:9

_____

_____

Ephesians 4:31-32

_____

_____

Romans 12:9-13

_____

_____

1 Peter 1:22-23

_____

_____

1 John 3:18-20

_____

_____

11. Through the power of God as reflected in the verses above, how might this rivalry have been transformed into God's love for one another?

And yet, even though Leah was unloved by Jacob, God exalted her by giving her many sons. Two of which would become the priestly and kingly tribes of Levi and Judah.

Family Traits

Joseph inherited many of his ancestors' best traits and characteristics, such as his strength of faith from Abraham, his patience and gentleness from Isaac, and his warmhearted and affectionate nature from his father, Jacob. As you read the scriptures concerning Joseph, look for these traits and others in his character.

Examine the following spiritual values of Joseph's family. Notice a common thread throughout this family line. Each person had a relationship with God, and they all believed His promises. Joseph had a mighty example of faith in the one true God from his great-grandfather, his grandfather and his father. Passing down the stories of faith and the covenant would have been told around the fire at night, during the day and during restful moments when opportunity arose for sharing their faith. Joseph would have heard and remembered such stories.

Spiritual Values of Joseph's Family			
Abraham	Isaac	Jacob	Joseph
Talked to God	Talked to God	Talked to God	Lived his faith
Man of Faith	Man of Faith	Wrestled with God	Man of Faith
Believed God's Promises	Believed God's Promises	Believed God's Promises	Believed God's Promises
Name changed by God		Name changed by God	
Friend of God			

Spiritual Values of Joseph's family

Negative traits are often passed down to subsequent generations as well. Joseph's family was no different. A pattern of scheming and deceitfulness can be found throughout his lineage. Examine the Negative Family Traits below for the ones found in Joseph's family. As you study the life of Joseph, become aware of these negative traits and determine if these traits were passed to Joseph and/or his brothers.

Negative Family Traits			
Abraham	Isaac	Jacob	Jacob's Sons
Along with Sarah schemed to "help" God with His promise of a child resulting in Hagar giving birth to Ishmael Genesis 16 Deceived Pharaoh and Abimelech concerning Sarah Genesis 12:10-20 Genesis 20:1-18	Schemed to "violate" God's revelation by blessing Esau, his favored son but was himself deceived Genesis 27:1-4 Rebekah schemed to help her favored son Jacob receive the blessing Genesis 27:5-40 Isaac deceived Abimelech concerning Rebekah Genesis 26:1-11	Jacob deceived his father and cheated his brother Genesis 27:11-29 Jacob deceived by Laban when Leah took Rachael's place as Jacob's bride Genesis 29:16-30	Jacob's sons deceived their father by claiming Joseph had been killed by an animal Genesis 37:18-35 Simeon and Levi deceive the Shechemites Genesis 34

Negative Family Traits

As you think about Joseph's family history of good and bad traits, consider the possibility of similar traits in your family. Use the following exercise as a way to examine issues that may be causing barriers in your life. Avoid blaming your ancestors for any negative traits you may find. You may not be able to change your past but you can change your future by the power of the living God.

Positive Personal Family Traits			
Relationship	Physical	Emotional	Spiritual
Mother			
Father			
Maternal Grandmother			
Maternal Grandfather			
Paternal Grandmother			
Paternal Grandfather			

Personal Family Traits

It is comforting to know that when Jesus Christ is your Savior, you can change some negative family traits for yourself and for future generations. In Exodus 20:5-6, God gives the Israelites a stern warning concerning the worship of idols. This warning affected their descendants:

"You shall not bow down to them or worship them; for I, the Lord your God, am a jealous God, punishing the children for the sin of the fathers to the third and fourth generation of those who hate me, but showing love to a thousand [generations] of those who love me and keep my commandments".

The measure of a person's character is not what is passed down from previous generations. It is measured by what he or she leaves behind. Leave those you love a rich faith and trust in God. Your life could help provide an example of God's love to a thousand generations.

If you do not know Jesus Christ as your Savior, please ask Him into your heart. Ask Him to forgive your sins then accept His payment of the shedding of His blood on the cross for you. Proclaim Him Lord, receive His forgiveness, and pray the sinner's prayer on page 74.

God's plan for the rest of your life begins now. Trust Him daily, no matter the circumstances. Forget the things of the past and walk forward in the love of Christ. Use Paul's example when he said, "But one thing I do: forgetting what is behind and straining toward what is ahead, I press on toward the goal to win the prize for which God has called me heavenward in Christ Jesus." (Philippians 3:13b-14). Dig deep into His Word. Pray and listen carefully to His leading. As His child, He wants you to develop a close family relationship.

Children are not responsible for family sins but each for their own sin. If you belong to Christ, take to heart Romans 2:6: "God will give to each person according to what he has done".

1. List the common spiritual family traits you see from each one listed below:

Abraham: _____

Sarah: _____

Isaac: _____

Rebekah: _____

Jacob: _____

2. List the common negative family traits you see from each one listed below:

    Abraham: _____

    Sarah: _____

    Isaac: _____

    Rebekah: _____

    Jacob: _____

3. What positive family traits do you think were passed down to Jacob's sons?

4. What negative family traits do you think were passed down to Jacob's sons including Joseph?

5. Read Ezekiel 18:14-17. How does it apply to you?

6. What positive family traits have you received from your family lineage?

7. Do you have ancestors who believed in Jesus Christ? How do you know?

8. Write the Biblical principle found in Galatians 6:7-8 in the space provided.

_____

_____

_____

9. Why should this principle be important to you?

Joseph's Family Life

Jacob was a wealthy man, and his family grew large as God blessed him while he lived and worked for Laban. When it was time to go back home, Jacob took his wives and eleven sons and all his abundant possessions and left abruptly. Laban did not know of their departure until returning home after shearing sheep. After an encounter with Jacob, Laban returns home and the family travels on their way. Nearing Canaan, Jacob learns that his estranged brother Esau is coming to meet him. Since parting after the stolen blessing didn't end in pleasantries, Jacob is afraid. To his surprise Esau has forgiven him because God has also blessed Esau giving him a large family and possessions.

As the family nears Ephrath (Bethlehem), the pregnant Rachel gives birth to Benjamin with great difficulty and dies soon after the birth of her son. She is buried near the place of her death. Today her tomb is located within a Muslim cemetery in a walled enclave near the outskirts of Bethlehem.

1. List Jacob's twelve sons (Genesis 29:31-30:22, Genesis 35:16-18):

Leah's sons: _____

Rachel's sons: _____

Bilhah's sons: _____

Zilpah's sons: _____

A large family represented prestige in the community because it showed God's blessings, perpetuated the family line, ensured care of the elderly and their proper burial, and provided an heir to which all property and family responsibilities were given. In the case of this family, it also continued God's covenant and promises given to Abraham through which God would make a great nation and bring the promised Messiah.

In this culture, a person's name had a special meaning. Examine the names of the sons of Jacob carefully and see if you can determine a progression of emotions Rachel and Leah felt as each child is born.

Leah-the unloved sister:
Reuben, whose name means "see, a son" or "he has seen my misery"
Simeon, whose name means "hearing" or "one who hears"
Levi, whose name means "attached"
Judah, whose name means "I will praise the Lord"
Issachar, whose name means "reward"
Zebulun, whose name means "honor"

Zilpah, Leah's maid given to Jacob when Leah stopped bearing children for a season: Leah was considered the mother of Zilpah's children and named them:

Gad, whose name means "good fortune"
Asher whose name means "women will call me happy."

Bilhah, Rachel's maid given to Jacob to bear children for Rachel years before the birth of Joseph and Benjamin
Rachel was considered the mother of Bilhah's children and named them:

Dan, whose name means "God has vindicated me"
Naphtali, whose name means "my struggle"

Rachel-the most loved sister:
Joseph, which means "God has taken away my disgrace".
Benjamin-Rachel died shortly after naming this child "Ben-oni" which means son of my sorrow but Jacob changed his son's name to Benjamin, which means "son of my right hand."

2. After close examination of the meaning of the names above, state your opinion as you describe the feelings, mood, and hopes of Leah and Rachel at the time of each child's birth.

_____

_____

_____

_____

_____

Birthright

Jacob's family lived in a patriarchal society, which meant Jacob had total authority over all matters concerning the family. The patriarch played a powerful and important role and his decisions covered all aspects of family life including 1. All social matters: including associations with certain tribes or groups; 2. Economic matters: trading, growing crops, raising herds and flocks; 3. Military matters: including decisions of tribal alliances and enemies; 4. Spiritual matters: such as what gods or God to worship; and 5. Life and death issues: the ultimate judge and jury of the family.

The birthright was most often given to the first born child but in some cases due to actions of the first child or pleasure of the father, that tradition was not followed. For example, in the recorded history in Genesis, we find three examples of such actions. Esau and Jacob, Manasseh and Ephraim and the three oldest sons of Jacob were not given the birthright based solely on the birth order.

It was customary to give a double portion of the inheritance to the one receiving the birthright. If there were two sons, the estate would be divided into three parts and two of these parts would be given to the birthright son. If there were three sons, the estate would be divided into four parts, etc. Usually not only did this son receive the birthright but would also receive the blessing as well. This made the position for receiving the birthright and blessing very valuable.

Three of Jacob's sons forfeited the birthright because of their evil deeds, leaving the birthright decision up to Jacob. This pending decision caused jealousy and bitterness among the brothers who no longer would receive the birthright as well as among those that could possibly be next in line. Would Jacob choose Judah, son of Leah, or Joseph, firstborn son of his beloved wife Rachel?

3. Why was the birthright important?

4. Who was Jacob's firstborn son and why did he not receive the birthright? (Genesis 35:22, Genesis 49:3-4; 1 Chronicles 5:1)

5. Why were Levi and Simeon passed over for the birthright? (Genesis 34:1-35, 49:5-7)

Favoritism

Read Genesis 37:1-4

6. Define favoritism.

_____

_____

_____

_____

The Bible states that Jacob loved Joseph more than his other sons. Jacob openly showed favoritism toward Joseph by showering him with gifts. Joseph's brothers became jealous and bitter toward Joseph and hated him.

One gift that Jacob gave Joseph seemed to trigger the brothers' emotions: a beautiful coat of many colors. This particular garment may have been a full-length cloak with long sleeves and made of fine linen, possibly with a fringe scarf. The fabric was woven with expensive dyed threads. Only royalty would have worn such a magnificent garment.

Joseph must have looked stunning in his coat, but the sight of him also brought about anger and jealousy in his brothers. It would have enraged them to see Joseph in this coat because he would not have been able to work in the fields in such a magnificent garment. In their own minds, it indicated to them Jacob's intention of giving Joseph the birthright.

7. Why was Joseph the favorite son of Jacob? (Genesis 37:3)

8. Why did Joseph's brothers hate him? (Genesis 37:2-4)

9. What did Joseph's coat represent?

10. What kind of attitude do you suppose Joseph had while wearing his coat?

11. Do you think Joseph was prideful because of his father's favoritism?

12. How do you think Joseph provoked his brothers to jealousy?

13. How could Jacob have prevented dissention in his family?

14. Colossians 3:20-21 provides tips for improving parenting skills. List them here.

15. How does learning about the issues of the birthright and favoritism give you insight into the family dynamics in which Joseph grew up?

Joseph's Dreams

"In many and various ways, God spoke of old to our fathers" (Hebrews 1:1).

When a reference is made to a dream, it is often referred to as a series of thoughts, or images occurring during sleep. Dreams during Joseph's time had significant meaning and were thought to come from the divine realm. God often used dreams as a way to communicate to His people. Dreams were so important in scripture; they were mentioned 121 times throughout the Old and New Testaments.

The Bible records how God used dreams during Joseph's life to accomplish the plan He had for him and the people of Israel. At the age of seventeen, God gave Joseph and his family a prophecy they did not understand until much later. During his imprisonment, Joseph interpreted correctly the dreams of the cupbearer and the baker thus planting the seed for what was to come. God continued to use Joseph through dream interpretation for Pharaoh as he predicted the famine soon to devour the land. God showed His great power and His hand upon Joseph as He worked through Joseph to bring about His divine plan.

1. Write out Job 33:14-16.

2. From these verses in Job, describe how God speaks to men in the Old Testament. How does God speak to us today?

The types of dreams recorded in the Bible include prophetic dreams that required interpretation, warnings dreams concerning a coming event, dreams concerning the will of God and what someone should do, and dreams to encourage obedience to the Lord. Examine the following information for an overview of some recorded dreams in scripture.

Type of Dream	Who's Dream	Scripture Reference
Prophetic	Abraham's 2nd vision	Genesis 15
Warning	Abimelech's Dream	Genesis 20:3
Prophetic	Jacob's Ladder	Genesis 28:12
Will of God	Jacob's return to Canaan	Genesis 31:10-13
Prophetic	Joseph's Dreams	Genesis 37:5-11
Prophetic	Baker and Cupbearer	Genesis 40:5-8
Prophetic	Pharaoh's Dreams	Genesis 41
Encouragement	Gideon	Judges 7
Will of God/Call	Isaiah's Call	Isaiah 6
Will of God/Call	Ezekiel's Call	Ezekiel 1
Prophetic	Daniel's Visions	Daniel 8-12
Prophetic	Nebuchadnezzar's 1st Dream	Daniel 2
Warning	Joseph's Dream	Matthew 1:20-21
Will of God	Man from Macedonia	Acts 16:9-10
Prophetic	Revelation	Entire Book

Dreams in the Bible

3. Summarize the following scripture references of recorded dreams and list the purpose for which it was given:

Abimelech (Genesis 20:3): _____

Jacob (Genesis 28:12, 31:10-13): _____

Daniel (Daniel 2:19, 7:1-8): _____

Joseph (Matthew 1:20-21, 2:13): _____

Paul (Acts 23:11): _____

Joseph's dreams were prophetic. They gave Joseph a vision of what was to come, and he knew that God was with him even though he wasn't sure how God would take him from the pit to the fulfillment of the dreams. They also served as a reminder to his father and brothers when they learned that Joseph was vizier of Egypt that God's prophecies are true and it is He who knows all things.

As you think about Joseph's dreams, place yourself at the scene as Joseph tells his brothers about the two dreams he had. Imagine Joseph's thoughts as he tells the dreams and imagine the thoughts of his brothers as they listened.

Read Genesis 37:5-11.

4. In what manner do you think Joseph presented his dreams to his family?

5. Describe Joseph's first dream. What did it mean?

6. Describe Joseph's second dream. What did it mean?

7. Why would Joseph's brothers be angry and provoked to jealousy over the dreams?

8. How did Jacob react to Joseph's dreams?

9. Why do you think God gave Joseph these dreams?

Scripture doesn't say that Joseph, who was a teenage boy at the time of his dreams, was to communicate his dreams to his family. The inexperience of youth showed he lacked wisdom. Sometimes it is best to keep what God tells you to yourself especially if you have a prideful spirit.

Jealousy

Read Genesis 37:4-11.

We see from these verses that Joseph's brothers first saw that their father loved Joseph more than he did the others. The jealousy they felt because of this favoritism soon turned to bitterness that grew stronger as the days went by.

10. Define jealousy.

_____

_____

_____

_____

11. Describe how you think Joseph's brothers fit this definition of jealousy.

Bitterness

As jealousy begins to consume thoughts and actions, it rapidly turns to bitterness. Bitterness by the brothers as they witnessed the favoritism and love Jacob showered on Joseph was overwhelming.

12. Define bitterness and circle the words in the definition of bitterness that describe the brothers.

_____

_____

_____

13. How are jealousy and bitterness related?

Had Joseph's brothers dealt with their emotions openly with their father, perhaps their actions would have been different. Just like the brothers, we often find ourselves harboring a root of bitterness from something that has happened. Sometimes we had no control over the situation, but many times we are part of the problem by word or deed. The important issue is to remove any jealousy or bitterness quickly before it results in an action similar or worse than that of Joseph's brothers. Had the communication line been open to Jacob, would Jacob have treated them differently and would their reactions been different?

14. Has there ever been a time in your life when a root of bitterness caused you to act in a manner that wasn't Christian-like?

15. Do you hold a root of bitterness toward someone?

16. What situation caused you to have this bitterness?

17. Could a growing root of bitterness cause some people to commit crimes? Give an example that states your opinion.

Their bitterness grew more intense daily and became a deep-rooted anger that led to hatred. Eventually, they became so angry with Joseph they could not even speak to him.

Hate

18. Define hate.

_____

_____

_____

19. Underline the words in the following verses that refer to _hate_ felt by Joseph's brothers: "And his brothers saw that their father loved him more than all his brothers; and so they hated him and could not speak to him on friendly terms . . . then Joseph had a dream, and when he told it to his brothers, they hated him even more . . . so they hated him even more for his dreams and for his words . . . (and) his brothers were jealous of him, but his father kept the saying in mind". (Genesis 37:4-5,8,11)

Because of the strong jealousy and bitterness toward Joseph, hatred toward him developed into feelings of extreme hostility that soon would result in action.

20. In our own life, there can be times when the same emotions can overwhelm us. How can we prevent jealousy and bitterness from becoming hatred?

God's Word tells us in the following passages how we need to handle these situations.

21. In the following verses underline how God expects us to react when confronted with these emotions.

Ephesians 4:31-32: Get rid of all bitterness, rage and anger, brawling and slander, along with every form of malice. [32] Be kind and compassionate to one another, forgiving each other, just as in Christ God forgave you

Hebrews 12:15: See to it that no one falls short of the grace of God and that no bitter root grows up to cause trouble and defile many.

Romans 13:13-14 Let us behave decently, as in the daytime, not in carousing and drunkenness, not in sexual immorality and debauchery, not in dissension and jealousy. [14] Rather, clothe yourselves with the Lord Jesus Christ, and do not think about how to gratify the desires of the flesh

James 3:14 But if you harbor bitter envy and selfish ambition in your hearts, do not boast about it or deny the truth.

Fueled by Jacob's special treatment of Joseph, his brothers became jealous of their father's favorite child. Joseph's brothers allowed jealousy to become bitterness that took root and grew into raging hatred. Soon that hatred would become an action.

Sold into Slavery

Read Genesis 37:12-36.

Jacob had large flocks needing green pastures to graze so Jacob sent the brothers of Joseph to take the sheep to pasture near Shecham. When they didn't return in a timely manner, Jacob sent Joseph out to make sure all was well.

Joseph traveled to Shecham but did not find them there. He was searching the fields when he found a man who told him they had taken the sheep on to Dothan a short distance away.

Dothan had rich pastures and rolling hills desirable for grazing large numbers of sheep. From the top of these hills the valley could be seen for miles. It is here the brothers saw Joseph coming in the distance. As Joseph walked closer they could also see the magnificent coat he wore. This very coat represented such a bond of love and emotion between their father and Joseph that it once again made them angry. Soon the discussion concerning Joseph grew from laughter and snide remarks to diabolical talk of murder. The closer Joseph drew near to them the more they despised him.

The brothers' first thought had been to kill Joseph but Reuben spotted an old dry cistern near by and he had an idea. It wasn't hard to convince the others to share in his plan. Once Joseph arrived the brothers ripped off his coat and threw him in the cistern until they could decide what to do with him. Reuben's intention was to rescue Joseph later and take him home but he left to return to the fields and by the time he came back Joseph was already gone.

Since there was no way for Joseph to escape, the rest of the brothers sat down to eat a meal. They spotted a far away Ishmaelite caravan traveling near Dothan on the major trade route from Gilead to Egypt. It appeared to be a long caravan looking to be several miles long and made up of many people some of which they were certain would be traders since it was their custom to travel in this manner to sell their goods.

Watching as the caravan slowly moved across the horizon, they spotted the Midianite traders traveling within the Ishmaelite caravan. These men were known for dealing in the slave trade. At that moment, Judah devised a plan of his own that would solve the problem of what to do with Joseph. Instead of killing Joseph, they would sell him to the slave traders. Making the deal and receiving the slave price of silver for a healthy, young Hebrew boy seemed to be fair trade. Joseph would be out of their lives and if he died his blood would not be on their hands. The guilt would belong to someone else.

Joseph would walk in shackles and chains for thirty days to reach Egypt where he would be sold as a common slave. Because of the harsh conditions, many slaves died along the trade route and Joseph did not know if he would survive. But this he did know, his hope and dreams for a life with his family were gone. He did not understand why God allowed him to be sold as a slave, but as he would learn years later, it was all part of God's plan for his life.

1. Describe the emotions Joseph might have felt while he was at the bottom of the pit. Remember that he was able to hear his brothers talking.

2. What was Reuben's motive for suggesting Joseph be thrown in the pit? (Genesis 37:21-22)

3. What was Judah's solution for taking care of Joseph? Explain his reasoning. (Genesis 37:26-27)

4. What was the slave price the brothers received for selling Joseph into slavery? (Genesis 37:28)

5. How might Joseph have felt after being shackled and chained as a slave?

6. What was Reuben's reaction when he returned to the cistern and Joseph was not there? (Genesis 37:29-30)

Read Genesis 37:31-38

7. How did Joseph's brothers attempt to cover up their crime?

8. What did they tell Jacob?

9. How did Jacob react to the news about Joseph's death?

Jacob's heart was broken and he thought he would surely die. He would mourn for his son until the day came of news that Joseph was alive and living in Egypt.

In Potiphar's House

Read Genesis 39.

During this period of Egyptian history, the slave trade flourished. There were many slaves who were prisoners of war, but most entered Egypt just as Joseph did: through the slave trade. Some officials and private individuals of wealth and position owned slaves. Potiphar was one such individual.

When Potiphar bought Joseph, he served as a household slave. He performed many common tasks for his master, including bringing food and drink to him. This son of Jacob who had been pampered by his father was now at the beck and call of Potiphar and his wife doing menial task. He was learning humility as well as other valuable lessons.

The Hebrew language is very different from the Egyptian language and in order to understand and perform his given tasks, Joseph would have to learn to communicate with the people in the land he now lived. Joseph must have been a quick study to learn to speak and understand the complex Egyptian language and to further his skills of writing and accounting in the Egyptian style. Joseph was promoted to overseer of Potiphar's house and fields. In this position, he would have to be literate in order to perform the duties this job required in supervising everything Potiphar owned.

Joseph was responsible for Potiphar's finances as well as managing meals, entertainment, household furnishings, household slaves, transportation, farm animals, crops, and slave laborers for the fields. He truly learned the ins and outs of Egyptian life. Scriptures tell us that God was with Joseph in all he did and he prospered, as did Potiphar's house.

God was preparing Joseph for a much greater role in His service. God had a plan for Joseph that would take years of preparation and required

Joseph's faith to mature. Joseph took full advantage of his position as slave. He didn't know why he was there, but he had decided that as long as God was with him, he would make the best of the situation.

1. What are some of the differences you imagine between life in Canaan and Egypt?

2. What common tasks do you think Joseph performed as a household servant before he became overseer of the estate?

3. How did Joseph's attitude affect his position in Potiphar's house?

4. Write down the following scriptures:

   Psalm 37:7

   _____
   _____
   _____
   _____

   Proverbs 15:13,15

   _____
   _____
   _____
   _____

5. Based on these scriptures, what attitude should we have in circumstances over which we have no control?

6. What was it that others saw in Joseph?

7. If you were placed in a situation similar to Joseph, would others see the same traits in you that they saw in Joseph?

8. Do you have a current job or situation that is making you unhappy or stressed?

9. How can you make the best of any situation for God's glory?

Resisting Temptations

Soon Potiphar's wife began to notice Joseph, he was forbidden to be with her. And this seemed to make him all the more appealing. He would move about the house all during the day. She began to find herself thinking of small tasks that he could do just to be near him. Every time he came near she would move close to him and smile. As time went by, day after day she would tease him and her lust for him grew stronger.

When scriptures say Potiphar's wife "cast lustful eyes on Joseph", we can know that lust had consumed her and she would try her very best to take it to the next level. First, a glance or two, then innocent laughter and jokes and soon she made plans to put her lust into action. Because she was Potiphar's wife and mistress of the house, she was used to getting her way. She gave an order and a slave carried it out. The more she looked, the more her lustful heart longed for him. She made several suggestive remarks to Joseph, but he refused her each time.

Then one day, she sent the other servants away so she was alone with Joseph. Once more she teased him, hoping this time she would overpower his will and his keen sense of right and wrong. Once more he reminded her of his God and her husband.

As she grabbed his coat, Joseph turned and ran away. In her anger for being rebuked, she accused Joseph of rape as she held "evidence" of his actions in her hands. Joseph said nothing in his defense, and Potiphar sent Joseph to prison in shackles.

10. What did Joseph say to Potiphar's wife? (Genesis 39:8-9)

11. How did Joseph prepare himself for her advances? (Matthew 26:41)

12. How did Joseph's rebuke of Potiphar's wife show his faith?

Read 1 Corinthians 10:12-13

13. What was Joseph's way out? How did Joseph act in the correct manner?

14. When Potiphar heard the story of what happened to his wife, was he right to believe his wife?

15. Under Egyptian law, Joseph could have been put to death. Why do you think Potiphar sent Joseph to prison instead of executing him?

16. Was Potiphar justified in sending Joseph to prison?

17. Have you ever been accused of something you didn't do?

This world is not fair, but God's justice will prevail. Joseph could have felt sorry for himself and blamed God for what was happening to him, but instead he chose to make the most of another bad situation. God had other things to teach Joseph before he would be released from prison and the prophetic dreams would be fulfilled.

Joseph in Prison

Read Genesis 39:20-Genesis 40

Being thrown in prison for a crime he did not commit was a devastating blow for Joseph. How could someone do what was right and still be punished? Had God forsaken Joseph? Was this where he was to die? What about the dreams? Had Joseph been wrong all along?

What Joseph learned in this situation was that his only option was to trust that God still was in control. He could feel sorry for himself or make the best of the situation. He found assurance in knowing that God was in control as he had been in the past.

Joseph was placed in the king's prison. The king's prison held many types of prisoners but held mostly prisoners that were political enemies or members of his court having done something to displease the Pharaoh.

The prison itself was most likely near Potiphar's house or close by since he was captain of the guard. These prisons were called round houses or house of round because of their shape. It looked like an upside down bowl buried in the ground. There were narrow windows at the top for air and light but make no mistake; it was a prison with dim light and stale air.

The warden of the prison recognized that there was something special about Joseph. What he discovered was Joseph's faith in the God who blessed him and all those around him. The warden assigned Joseph to be in charge of all things concerning the operation of the prison supervised only by him. Putting Joseph in charge of the prisoners was exactly where God had intended.

Once again Joseph found himself in a leadership position in a place that was not his choice. But with a right attitude and God's help, Joseph would learn many lessons of leadership and responsibility in providing for those who could not take care of themselves. He had an opportunity to learn compassion for the less fortunate and it gave him an opportunity to share his faith in God.

Joseph would have the opportunity to meet the baker and the cupbearer, two prisoners from Pharaoh's court that somehow had displeased the king. Unbeknownst to him, dreams would play an important role in Joseph's life and the solution to being released from prison.

One morning as Joseph went to check on each prisoner, he noticed the baker and the cupbearer were distressed. Asking why, each one explained they had a dream and didn't know what the dream meant. Joseph reminded them God is the one who gives interpretation. Joseph listened carefully and told each of them their dream meaning. In three days, the baker would die and the cupbearer would be restored to his former position with Pharaoh. Joseph instructed the cupbearer to remember him when he was restored to Pharaoh's court. The dreams were fulfilled but Joseph was not remembered.

It is here in this place that God would continue teaching Joseph and preparing him for yet another position. Joseph still had much to learn before God's ultimate plan could be carried out. In prison, Joseph would learn more about Egyptian life and Pharaoh's court. These lessons would prepare him for the job of vizier of Egypt and be valuable skills in coming days.

1. Write down the following scriptures:

Philippians 4:11-13

_____

_____

_____

_____

1 Thessalonians 5:18

_____

_____

_____

_____

2. Using the above scripture, what do you think was Joseph's attitude in prison?

3. With whom did Joseph find favor while in prison? (Genesis 39:21)

4. What gifts and talents do you think Joseph had that were recognized while he was in prison? (Genesis 39:21-23)

5. How did God use the chief cupbearer and chief baker's dreams to prepare the way for His plan for Joseph? (Genesis 41:9)

6. Joseph waited two years for the cupbearer to remember him. If you were Joseph, what would you have thought about the cupbearer after such a long period of time had elapsed?

7. How did Joseph respond when the cupbearer forgot to mention him to Pharaoh?

8. Was there ever a time in your life when it seemed that God wasn't listening to your prayers but then His answers came at precisely the right time? What was it?

9. What did Joseph need to learn while in prison? What had he learned up to that point?

10. What skills and characteristics do you think Joseph would need to serve in the position of vizier? Do an Internet search for the duties of Egypt's vizier.

_____

_____

Pharaoh's Dreams

Read Genesis 41:1-40

Two long years had passed as Joseph waited for the cupbearer to remember him for interpreting his dream. He had agreed to mention Joseph's situation to the Pharaoh but nothing happened. Joseph continued his everyday responsibilities doing the very best he could in the situation he found himself.

Meanwhile, the cupbearer was enjoying his reinstated position in Pharaoh's court and had completely forgotten Joseph until one morning when something unusual happened. Very early Pharaoh, looking distraught, called all of his wise men, magicians and other consult to appear before him. As he spoke to his court, the cupbearer was serving drink and overheard all that was said.

Pharaoh had two dreams on the same night that greatly distressed him. Having given every detail of the two dreams, he waited for an interpretation from his most trusted group of seers. They had interpreted dreams before and surely their explanation would be correct. They consulted together discussing the dreams and arguing back and forth for what seemed a long time. Pharaoh grew impatient giving orders to tell him the meaning now. But they could not interpret these dreams. Pharaoh was clearly angry.

These learned men were experts in their craft. They had trained in understanding and interpreting dreams from the "dream books" that had provided "scientific" documentation concerning past dreams and interpretations. Yet with these particular dreams, they could not understand the meaning.

Observing Pharaoh's growing anger and having no particular love for the seers the cupbearer wondered why these men that were suppose to be so smart and the "most learned" men in the nation couldn't figure out the interpretation. It was at that moment the cupbearer remembered Joseph. Humbly, the cupbearer approached Pharaoh and told him of the experience he had while in prison. He explained his dream and that of the baker and a man called Joseph who had interpreted their dreams correctly.

Pharaoh demanded Joseph be brought to him quickly. God was about to bring Joseph to the place He had been preparing him over the last thirteen years.

1. Who did Pharaoh first call to interpret his dreams? (Genesis 41:8)

2. Why did Pharaoh call these men?

3. What did Egyptians believe about dreams?

4. Why was Joseph called to appear before Pharaoh? (Genesis 41:9-13)

When Joseph received word that Pharaoh wanted his appearance in his court, his heart skipped a beat. Was he finally going to be heard? Had the cupbearer finally remembered him and now he might be able to prove his innocence?

Thinking he was called before Pharaoh because of his own situation, Joseph had no idea what would happen. Pharaoh had the power of life and death and he did not know for sure if this was the time when his life would end. Joseph was nervous and filled with anxiety. He prayed and he prayed hard.

5. Why did Joseph bathe and clean up after he was summoned to see Pharaoh? (Genesis 41:14)

Prison was a dirty place and Joseph was filthy, smelly and his beard, his hair and his body had not been clean for a while. Lest he offend the Pharaoh's keen sense of cleanliness, Joseph first had to bath, shave and dress in clean clothing.

As Joseph arrived in Pharaoh's presence, he bowed humbly and listened carefully as Pharaoh himself was speaking. Pharaoh explained that he had two dreams that no one could interpret and he was told that Joseph could interpret dreams.

Joseph respectfully said to Pharaoh that he could not interpret them but God would give Pharaoh the answers he desired. Joseph listened carefully as Pharaoh revealed his dreams. Joseph replied that God had told Pharaoh what he was about to do and Joseph told him the meaning of the dreams. God would give seven years of abundant harvest to Egypt followed by seven years of famine. This was firmly decided by God and would come about soon.

6. What were the interpretations of Pharaoh's dreams? (Genesis 41:25-39)

7. According to the interpretations, how would Egypt be saved? (Genesis 41:33-36)

Joseph continued to tell Pharaoh what he needed to do for the nation to survive the famine. He suggested to Pharaoh that he chose a wise and discerning man to oversee the harvesting and storing of grain in the cities during the years of abundance. This grain could then be used during the famine to feed the starving.

8. What was Pharaoh's response to the interpretations and how did it affect Joseph? (Genesis 41:37-41)

Pharaoh approved of the plan and since he could not think of anyone any wiser than Joseph, he appointed him vizier of Egypt. He was given authority over all the land and the only one with more power than Joseph would be the Pharaoh himself.

9. What gifts did Pharaoh bestow on Joseph? (Genesis 41:44-46)

10. What name did Pharaoh give to Joseph? (Genesis 41:45)

Joseph was given the Egyptian name Zaphenath-Paneah, the Pharaoh's signet ring for signing official documents was placed on his finger and he was dressed in the finest linen garments. The gold collar of authority was placed around his neck and he was given his own chariot to ride behind Pharaoh. To give him more credibility as an Egyptian, he was also given the daughter of Potiphera, priest of On as a wife! And then Pharaoh put him in charge of all of Egypt.

What an amazing turn of events! Joseph could have never imagined he would be appointed to such an important position. God had brought him to His intended place and Joseph was grateful. Remembering his dreams, Joseph began to understand in a small way why he was there. It would be many years before he would understand completely.

11. How old was Joseph when he became vizier of Egypt? (Genesis 41:46)

Vizier of Egypt! What a surprise. From favorite son to slave, from prison to palace, it had to be a divine plan. No human could have ever planned such an event. Joseph's work was about to begin. If he had learned all the lessons God had prepared along his years of trials and struggles, he would be successful.

He would depend on God now as he had in the past. Joseph believed God had been with him from the beginning moments of his journey and was protecting and providing for him. Joseph knew God had never forsaken him. He realized now the huge task set before him, but Joseph knew God most certainly was there and would guide him in the saving of many lives from starvation.

Read 1 Samuel 7 (the story of the Ebenezer stone), which recounts a time when the Israelites were reminded of God's protection and blessings.

12. What does the word "Ebenezer" mean?

13. What significance was the stone to the Israelites?

14. How would you apply this to Joseph's situation and yours?

The Fat and the Famine

Read Genesis 41:41-57

The fulfillment of Pharaoh's dreams meant seven years of plenty followed by seven years of famine. The manner in which Joseph prepared and executed his plan during the time of plenty would determine the number of people who survived. Joseph would need God's wisdom and guidance more than ever. He listened carefully to what the Lord instructed as he carried out God's plan.

1. What did he do to prepare for the famine? (Genesis 41:46-49)

Joseph traveled the countryside of Egypt visiting cities and fields to determine what Egypt already had in the way of fields of harvest and sites of existing storage facilities.

He became very familiar with every part of Egypt including the delta area near the Nile River. Fertile soil and seasonal flooding provided excellent conditions for growing crops and it was here that most of the wheat, barley and other food crops were grown. Since cities also grew first along the Nile, Joseph most likely would choose the locations for his new storage units to accommodate the abundant harvest near the river.

Joseph must know exactly how much grain they gathered. He had scribes stationed at each storage facility to record exact amounts of grain inventory. These scribes kept detailed accounts until the abundance was so great they could not count it all. The grain was described as being as abundant as the sands of the sea and beyond measure. And Joseph stopped counting.

Joseph worked diligently to carry out the task of preparing for the coming famine. God had blessed him as administrator with discernment and wisdom. Joseph was able to complete this huge task of preparation before the seven-year famine began.

2. Write down the following scriptures:

Proverbs 16:3

_____
_____
_____
_____

Proverbs 19:21

_____
_____
_____
_____

Isaiah 23:9

_____
_____
_____
_____

Isaiah 30:1

_____
_____
_____
_____

3. Using the scriptures above, how are we to plan and work for God?

4. How do these scriptures apply to your life?

Joseph sought God's guidance in preparing for the famine and God prospered him. Because of Joseph's willingness to be obedient to God's leading, many lives were saved from starvation.

During the seven years of plenty, God continued to bless Joseph.

5. What gifts did God give to Joseph? (Genesis 41:50-52)

God had not forgotten Joseph's heart and He blessed him with two sons during these same years of abundance. Joseph named his firstborn son Manasseh because "God had made me forget all my trouble and all my father's household". Joseph was now in a place in his life that he could forgive what his family had done to him and rejoice in this new life God provided.

Joseph's second son was named Ephraim because; "God has made me fruitful in the land of my suffering." In spite of everything Joseph had been through from the time he was sold into slavery until now, he realized that God was blessing him right here in the land of Egypt with another precious son.

The seven years of famine came all to soon. Even though Egypt was prepared, the famine was devastating. The Egyptians began feeling the effects of the famine and petitioned Pharaoh for food. Joseph opened the storehouses and sold grain to the people of all countries because the famine was very severe in all the lands.

6. When the famine came, what could Joseph do for the people of Egypt and other countries? (Genesis 41:53-57)

Read Genesis 47:13-26

7. What did Joseph do with the money he collected for grain? (Genesis 47:13-14)

8. When all the Egyptians ran out of money to buy grain, how did Joseph sell them food? (Genesis 47:15-17)

9. Once the livestock all belonged to Pharaoh, what did the people give to buy grain? (Genesis 47:18-21)

10. What was the stipulation concerning the seed given to the Egyptian people to plant? (Genesis 47:23-26)

By the time the famine was over, Pharaoh owned most of the land and people in Egypt. The only people whose land, livestock and very lives did not belong to Pharaoh were the priests. They had been spared because they received a regular allotment from Pharaoh.

Meanwhile, in the land of Canaan, Jacob and his family were feeling the effects of the famine. Jacob was planning to send ten sons to Egypt to buy food to feed the family. Little did Joseph know that one of the greatest desires of his heart would soon be fulfilled: seeing his father again.

Joseph and His Brothers

Read Genesis 42

Famine caused great hunger and starvation in Egypt and other nations, including Canaan. Soon Jacob sent ten of his sons to Egypt to buy grain because he had heard reports that Egypt had an abundance of grain available for purchase.

The brothers prepared to make their way down to Egypt. Benjamin, the youngest and the only full brother of Joseph, stayed behind with Jacob. Jacob had become increasingly protective of Benjamin, the last living child of his beloved Rachel. He would not allow him to leave his side because he was afraid harm would come to him as it had to Joseph. Memories of Joseph were still active in Jacob's mind and his heart still ached as he thought of him.

As Joseph prepared to receive the lines of men coming to buy grain, he came face to face with the ten brothers who hated him. Suddenly the whole scene replayed in his mind. He saw them ripping off his coat and throwing him in the pit. He replayed the words they spoke and heard the tone of hatred in their voices. And then came the horrible feelings of despair he felt in the pit. It was almost more than he could bear.

He began to wonder as these same men bowed before him. Were they still the same jealous brothers filled with hatred that had wanted to kill Joseph? Were they the same brothers who hated him so much they sold him into slavery? Had their hearts changed at all?

As he pondered these thoughts his dreams came flashing back to mind. The dreams! Just now one dream has been fulfilled. The very first dream had come true just as predicted. God had revealed this dream to him at age seventeen and Joseph was beginning to understand God's plan for his life. Perhaps even a plan that included the covenant promise

God had given Abraham. This prophecy from God foretold Abraham's people would live in a strange land for four hundred years, be enslaved and then return home with great possessions.

Joseph could not tell them at this point who he was. No, he must wait until he discerned the matter of their heart. So he devised a test.

1. When did Joseph recognize his brothers and when did he remember his dreams? (Genesis 42:6-9)

2. How did Joseph treat his brothers and why? (Genesis 42:7-8)

3. What information did the brothers provide about their family? (Genesis 42:10-13)

Joseph treated the brothers as strangers and spoke harshly to them accusing them of being spies. This was a serious accusation for the brothers.

Because traders and ordinary people coming to purchase grain could move around unnoticed in a country, it was common practice for nations to send this type of men and women into a country to trade and observe where the weakest defenses of a country might lie. This information was then passed back to the king who paid for the information they gave. The penalty for spying had severe consequences which included deportation, beating and in some incidences death.

4. Why did Joseph not reveal his identity to his brothers immediately?

Joseph then makes a bold move. After accusing them of being spies, he proclaims their fate lies in one condition; one brother would be sent home to bring the youngest brother to Egypt while the others stayed in prison. If he returned with the youngest brother, the vizier would know they were telling the truth. He then sent them all to prison for three days.

5. Why did Joseph send them to prison for three days? (Genesis 42:15-17)

6. After spending time in prison, how did the brothers react? (Genesis 42:21-22)

7. Twenty years had gone by since Joseph was sold into slavery, so why would his brothers think they were being punished now?

8. Why did they blame each other? (Genesis 42:21)

9. What emotions did Joseph feel after his brothers were brought from prison? (Genesis 42:24)

At first, Joseph wanted to send only one of his brothers back for Benjamin and imprison the other nine. After his brothers spent three days in prison, Joseph revised his plan and sent all but one brother, Simeon, home with instructions to bring Benjamin to Egypt.

10. Why did Joseph imprison Simeon? (Genesis 42:24b)

As the brothers leave Egypt without Simeon, Joseph orders his servant to secretly place the silver they had used to purchase grain back into the sack of each brother. The servant gave them provisions for the trip and the brothers left to return home.

As they stopped for the night, one brother opened his sack to feed his donkey and found his silver in his sack. They all trembled with fright. The Egyptian was a hard man and they feared what he would do to them. They cried out "What is this God has done to us?" Upon returning home each brother finds silver in his sack as well. They were very afraid.

11. Why did Joseph have his servant put money in the brothers' grain sacks?

Jacob in disbelief is angry because of the demand of the man in Egypt. He declared Simeon and Joseph to be no more and refuses to let Benjamin return with the brothers. Reuben tries to make a bargain with Jacob but he refuses to allow Benjamin to make the trip back to Egypt.

12. What was Jacob's reaction when his sons came home without Simeon? (Genesis 42:35-36)

13. Why did Reuben plead for Benjamin to return with him to Egypt? (Genesis 42:37)

14. Why do you think Jacob was not persuaded by Reuben to send Benjamin to Egypt?

Some might think it strange for Joseph to test his brothers. Each of us is faced with situations when we do not know whether a family member, friend, or acquaintance is truthful and can be trusted. God gives us discernment to test the heart of others just as Joseph did.

To discern the heart of someone, you must be able to discover what is inside. Joseph could not look into his brothers' hearts, but he could provide a way to examine outward actions that indicated what was hidden within.

15. Write down the following scriptures that help us discern the hearts of someone else and underline what we need to look for as evidence of truth:

1 Corinthians 13:1-3:

_____
_____
_____
_____

Matthew 7:15-20:

_____
_____
_____
_____

Proverbs 15:14:

_____
_____
_____
_____

To help you discern the truth, remember to look for the outward action. A deceitful heart will give itself away. Joseph would discover soon whether or not his brothers truly were honest men with changed hearts.

Return to Egypt

Read Genesis 43

The famine was very severe and soon Jacob and his large family used all the grain that had been purchased in Egypt. Jacob noted this fact and he told his sons to go back down to Egypt and purchase more grain.

This time it was Judah that spoke up. He reminded Jacob of Joseph's demand having told them not to return unless the youngest brother was with them. Jacob still refusing to send Benjamin gets angry accusing the brothers of giving the man too much information.

Judah simply states that if Benjamin does not make the trip with them, they will not go and all the family will die. Judah pleads with Jacob to let Benjamin make the trip and pledges a guarantee of his safety. Judah tells his father that he will be responsible if something happens. Jacob must have heard something in his voice that told him this son was responsible enough to be trusted with his precious son Benjamin or perhaps thought he didn't have a choice. Jacob relents and agrees allowing Benjamin to accompany his brothers.

Jacob tells them to take gifts to the man in Egypt and perhaps he would think kindly of them. These gifts included products not commonly found in Egypt such as certain types of spices and food products. Jacob also insisted they take double the silver to replace what was found in the sacks from the first trip to Egypt and enough to purchase more grain.

Jacob sends them on their way with Benjamin and a prayer of blessing that God would grant them mercy before this hard man of Egypt. All ten of the brothers hurried down to Egypt to present themselves to Joseph.

1. Why was Judah able to convince Jacob to allow Benjamin to return with them to Egypt? (Genesis 43:1)

2. Why did Jacob finally let Benjamin return to Egypt with his brothers? (Genesis 43:1-10)

3. What other gifts besides spices, did the brothers take with them to Egypt for the vizier? (Genesis 43:11-15)

As the brothers make the trip to Egypt, they were uneasy and anxious about what would happen. Will this man believe they did not steal the silver? Will he let Simeon out of prison? Will he believe they had been telling the truth? If not, what kind of fate would they receive? Was God going to punish them further for what they had done to Joseph?

Joseph saw them coming. He strained his eyes to see if Benjamin was with them. Then he caught a glimpse of him. He recognized him immediately in spite of the fact that he had been so young the last time he saw him. He was so handsome. He looked like his beautiful mother. Joseph's heart skipped a beat. Finally, he would be near his brother but could not tell him just yet who he was.

Joseph told his servant to make preparations for dinner for the brothers would be coming to Joseph's house. He also gave him instructions on how to set the table arrangements and then instructed him to take the brothers directly to his house.

Terror filled their hearts as the servant told them they would be going to the vizier's house. Whispers rushed quickly between them. Is he going to overpower us and take our donkeys and make us slaves? He thinks we stole the silver we had brought the first time. They felt a range of emotions, from fear to astonishment, as they arrived at the vizier's house.

The brothers told the servant the silver was found in their sacks on the return trip back home when one of them opened the sack to feed the animals. The servant didn't seem concerned and simply said to their amazement, I have your money; your God must have put it there. This was turning out to be an unusual day.

Joseph arrived home and everyone was seated in the appropriate place. Joseph had his own table apart from anyone else due to his exalted position of authority. The other Egyptian guests had a separate table because they could not eat at the same table with men such as these unclean brothers who tended sheep. Joseph's brothers, including Simeon who had been brought from prison, sat at their table and were astonished their places were set in their birth order beginning with Rueben and ending with Benjamin. How could anyone know this information?

Joseph sent food from his dinner table to the brothers but gave Benjamin five times more than the others. Everyone ate and drank to their heart's content. They really didn't know what to make of how the vizier was treating them, and they certainly never guessed the vizier was their brother Joseph.

Joseph watched very carefully to see if there was even the slightest hint of jealousy toward Benjamin. He observed the looks in their eyes, the words from their mouths and the gestures they made. He saw nothing that would indicate their attitudes were based on jealousy and hatred.

To truly know their hearts concerning Benjamin, Joseph devised a final test.

4. How were the brothers treated when they returned to Egypt? (Genesis 43:16-17)

5. Why were the brothers afraid? (Genesis 43:17-23)

6. What did Joseph's servant say to the brothers to alleviate their fears? (Genesis 43:23-25)

7. What did Joseph do when his emotions overcame him? (Genesis 43:29-30)

8. Describe the seating arrangement at the brothers' dinner table. (Genesis 43:32-34)

9. Why were shepherds and Egyptians not allowed to eat together? (Genesis 43:32)

10. Why did Benjamin receive five times as more food as the others? (Genesis 43:34)

The Final Test

Read Genesis 44:1-34

After dinner, eleven brothers took their leave for the night and prepared to return home in the morning with full sacks of grain. The mood was a merry one. Everyone is back together and all is well. Jacob would see his son Benjamin again.

Unbeknown to the sons of Jacob, Joseph had told his servant to place the silver the brothers had brought to pay for the grain back into their individual sacks. In addition, he was to place in Benjamin's sack Joseph's special silver cup. The disappearance of Joseph's silver cup would cause grave consequences. To steal from one with such power would surely bring death.

If the brothers wanted an excuse to get rid of Benjamin like they had Joseph, this would be a simple solution. Benjamin would be left in Egypt for stealing the cup, and the others would return home to their families. Their reaction to this situation would determine what they had in their heart. Would they leave Benjamin knowing Jacob would mourn to death or would they all give themselves to the vizier to be imprisoned, made slaves, or executed? Would Joseph's revenge be complete or did he have a forgiving heart?

1. What was Joseph's plan to determine whether his brothers' hearts were true and free of hatred?(Genesis 44:1-2)

2. Explain what happened when Joseph's brothers began the trip back to Canaan. (Genesis 44:3-13)

3. What was the consequence of stealing from the Egyptian court? (Genesis 44:10, 16-17)

When the servant caught up with the brothers accusing them of stealing, they were dumbfounded in disbelief. Positive the servant would find nothing in their sacks to support this accusation, they offered to kill the one whose sack revealed the cup and the rest of them would instantly become slaves.

When Benjamin's sack revealed the stolen cup, they tore their clothes in mourning, loaded their donkeys and returned to the city with Joseph's servant. Disbelief and fear filled their souls.

Joseph was still in his house when his brothers returned. They threw themselves on the ground and trembled before him. Joseph spoke angrily to them and they trembled all the more. Surely this man would make all of them slaves and execute Benjamin.

Judah spoke humbly to Joseph, stating that God had uncovered their guilt and all of them would be his slaves including the one found with the cup. But Joseph refused and said only the one found with the cup would be the slave. The rest may go home.

Judah then speaks to Joseph recounting the events up to this time concerning the situation between their father and Benjamin and how Jacob would die if Benjamin did not return. Judah then offers himself to stay in place of Benjamin to relieve the guilt and blame he would bear if anything happened to this son who was so entwined with his father's soul.

4. What were Judah's motives in offering himself to remain in Benjamin's place? (Genesis 44:18-34)

5. How did Joseph know his brothers' hearts had changed?

Read Genesis 45:1-24.

Joseph now could see their true hearts. The jealousy and hatred had long passed and the feeling they had for Benjamin and Jacob were different. At this point, Joseph could no longer control his emotions. He sent all the servants away and he wept. He wept so loudly the Egyptians and Pharaoh's household heard him. The brothers sat terrified. This man of authority was wailing. And then the words that came next were unbelievable.

Joseph's words "I am Joseph." rang in their ears and their hearts melted. How could that be? He was sold as a slave. How could he become second in command of the great land of Egypt. They were terrified and could not even speak.

Joseph spoke again. "I am Joseph. The one you sold into Egypt!" and then he said these words, "Do not be distressed and do not be angry with yourselves. God sent me to save your lives and the lives of many people. It was not you who sent me here, but God."

6. After Judah pleaded for Benjamin's life, what did Joseph do (Gen. 45:1)?

7. What was Joseph's first question to his brothers after he declared who he was? (Genesis 45:3)

8. How did Joseph's words reflect forgiveness for what the brothers had done? Explain your answer.

9. How many times did Joseph mention God's name in Genesis 45 and what is the significance of this?

Joseph explained how God had blessed him. He instructed them to go home and return to Egypt with his father and live in the region of Goshen to be near him and he would take care of them through the coming years of famine. The brothers still sat in disbelief and said nothing. Joseph drew Benjamin close to him and said, "Look. See the resemblance between Benjamin and myself. Look at our eyes. Are they not the same?"

Joseph threw his arms around his brother Benjamin and wept. Benjamin embraced him and they wept together. Joseph then kissed each brother and wept over them. Finally, the brothers talked openly to their brother they hated so many years ago and the healing began.

Pharaoh gave permission for Joseph's family to move to Egypt and provided them with carts for Jacob and the small children in which to ride on the return trip to Egypt. Pharaoh's instructions were to gather everyone up, leave your possessions behind because he would provide for them with the best things Egypt had to offer when they returned.

Joseph gave them abundant provisions for the return trip home. Soon he would see his father again and rejoice.

10. How did Pharaoh react to the news of Joseph's family? (Genesis 45:16-20)

11. What were the provisions Joseph provided for the trip home? (Genesis 45:21-23)

12. What were the last words Joseph said to his brothers before they left for Canaan and why did he say it? (Genesis 45:24)

A Family Reunion

Read Genesis 46:1-30

Joseph's brothers arrived in Canaan with a caravan full of goods that Joseph had provided. Jacob saw the caravan coming from a long distance away. He was anxious to see if Benjamin was among them. Finally spotting Benjamin as they drew closer, his heart was relieved. He didn't understand the abundance of carts and supplies and began to wonder why so many were coming his way.

Benjamin was so excited to tell his father about Joseph his speech was too fast for Jacob to understand. All the brothers chimed in and that only made matters worse. Finally, Judah explained Joseph is alive and he told Jacob everything Joseph had said. Jacob was stunned. He did not believe them. But when they showed him all that Joseph had sent and the carts to return him to Egypt, Jacob was convinced. Joseph was alive! And he wanted desperately to see his son before he died.

1. Explain Jacob's emotions and his reaction to the news about Joseph. (Genesis 45:26-28)

Jacob had longed to see his precious son and hold him in his arms since the day they brought his blood stained coat to him and placed it in his hands. Now that he knew Joseph was alive and living in Egypt, he knew he must see him. Jacob had decided to make the trip to Egypt, but first he had to stop at Beersheba.

2. Why was it important for Jacob to stop at Beersheba? (Genesis 46:1)

3. What did God tell Jacob while in Beersheba? (Genesis 46:2-4)

4. What promise did God give Jacob concerning Joseph? (Genesis 46:4)

After confirming his decision to travel to Egypt, the family started off on the long trip. Jacob's entire family and all their possessions moved with them so it was a very long procession. Jacob and the children rode in the carts provided by Pharaoh. The others walked or rode their donkeys surrounded by all their livestock. Jacob was so anxious to see his lost son that the journey seemed as if it would never end.

5. How many people moved to Egypt with Jacob and how many total members of his family were counted as living there? (Genesis 46:26-27)

6. Why was it important to know the exact number of Jacob's people living in Egypt at this time?

Just after they entered Egypt, Jacob sent Judah ahead to ask Joseph directions to Goshen, the place where they would settle. Joseph was ready and anxiously awaiting word of his family. His chariot was prepared and ready to head out at a moments notice. Knowing that his father was near, Joseph could not wait another second and immediately started out to meet up with the father he had longed to see for so many years. This meeting was a special moment when the two remembered the years apart and had the joy of experiencing the delight of being reunited.

7. Describe Joseph and Jacob's reunion. (Genesis 46:28-30)

8.   What were Jacob's first words to Joseph? (Genesis 46:30)

Read Genesis 46:31-47:12

The Bible does not state the entire family bowed down before Joseph. But because of the exalted position Joseph held and because it was protocol for anyone coming before his presence to do so, most likely this would have taken place the moment they meet him. At this point Joseph's second dream would have been fulfilled.

After the safe arrival of his family, Joseph informed them that he must go meet with Pharaoh and let him know his family had arrived. Joseph took five of his brothers and his father dand presented them to Pharaoh. Pharaoh asked their occupation and they answered, as instructed by Joseph, they were shepherds. Permission was granted for all to live in Goshen. Since Pharaoh needed someone to care for his own sheep, he asked if any of the family had special ability in caring for livestock. What an honor to care for Pharaoh's own flocks!

9.   Describe the land of Goshen. (Genesis 47:1-6)

10. Why would God have His people live in Goshen? (Genesis 46:3)

Joseph presented his father Jacob to Pharaoh and Jacob blessed Pharaoh. Pharaoh was fascinated with Jacob's advanced age asking him how old he was. He answered that he was one hundred and thirty years old but his fathers had been much older. Because the Egyptians average life span was between thirty to forty years old, someone much older than those years was thought to be evidence of special divine favor and rewarded with a long life because of blameless behavior. Jacob again blessed Pharaoh and returned to Goshen where he would live the rest of his life.

Joseph gave his family the best land in Egypt and took care of them providing food during the remaining years of the famine.

11. How long did Jacob live in Goshen? (Genesis 47:28)

Blessings and Burial

Read Genesis 48 and 49

God had changed Jacob's name to Israel when Jacob wrestled with God in Genesis 32:22-32. Moving to Egypt was God's design. He would separate them from the Egyptians and grow their number. It is here they would become a large nation. Jacob's descendants would be known as the children of Israel.

Before Jacob died, he called Joseph and his sons to his bedside. He blessed Joseph and adopted his sons as his own. Then he blessed Ephraim and Manasseh. This gave Joseph a double portion of the Promised Land as the right of one who has been given the birthright.

1. What did it mean for Jacob to bless Ephraim with his right hand? (Genesis 48:17-20)

2. What blessings did Jacob give Joseph? (Genesis 48:12-22)

Jacob called for all his sons to come to his bedside where he pronounced the blessing for each one.

3. Two of his sons _____ and _____ did not receive the blessing of the land. One did not receive land at all and the other son received a small portion that was carved out of Judah's inheritance.

4. What was the reason Jacob did not give these two sons land of their own? (Genesis 49:5-7, Genesis 38)

5. Which son received the birthright? (Ezekiel 47:13, 1 Chronicles 5:1-2)

6. Why was Reuben passed over for the birthright? (Genesis 35:22, Genesis 49:3-4, 1 Chronicles 5:1-2)

7. Which son was given a blessing that included a prophecy of the Messiah (Genesis 49:8-9)?

After Jacob had given all of his sons the pronouncement of the blessings, he gave instructions for his burial. He had already made Joseph swear an oath to bury him in the burial place of his fathers.

Read Genesis 50:1-14

8. Where was the location of the burial place Jacob requested for his buried? (Genesis 49:29-30)

9. Who was buried in this place? (Genesis 49:31)

10. Why do you think Jacob had made Joseph swear an oath for his burial place and then also gave instructions to the other sons as well?

11. How old was Jacob when he came to Egypt? (Genesis 47:9) _____ How many years had he lived in Goshen? (Genesis 47:28) _____ How old was Jacob when he died? _____

12. How did Joseph react to Jacob's death? (Genesis 50:1)

13. How was Jacob's body prepared for burial and why do you think this method was chosen? (Genesis 50:1-3)

Because Joseph was a very important man, all of Egypt mourned for his father. Jacob was given the rights of a dignitary and when the procession left Egypt to travel to the final burying place, a very large number accompanied him.

14. Name the groups of people that were included in Jacob's processional? (Genesis 50:7-9)

God had told Jacob to go down to Egypt and live with his family and now Joseph was bringing him back home. When they reached the threshing floor of Atad near the Jordan River the procession stopped. They were no longer in Egypt.

Such a large group of loud wailing people, who looked like Egyptians, attracted the attention of the Canaanites living in the area. Thinking they were invaders they came to see what was happening. Realizing there was no danger, the Canaanites left them in peace to mourn.

15. What are some other reasons besides mourning, the procession might have stopped at Atad? (Genesis 50:10)

With the burial of their father complete, Joseph and his brothers as well as the others who had accompanied them returned to Egypt. Now the brothers would begin to think about the consequences of their past actions.

Forgiveness

Read Genesis 50:15-21

Jacob died when he was 147 years old. Joseph, as promised, took Jacob's body back to Canaan to be buried in the cave at Machpela. After Jacob's death, Joseph faced another situation involving his brothers.

Thinking perhaps the only reason Joseph tolerated them was because of their father who was now dead, the brothers spent many hours talking among themselves concerning what they had done to Joseph. Daring not to appear in person and so uncertain as to the feelings of Joseph toward them, they send a messenger to Joseph. In the message, the brothers claimed that before he died, Jacob asked for Joseph to forgive them for what they had done to him.

1. Do you believe this message was a true request from Jacob or one the brothers made up? Give reasons for your opinion.

2. Why do you think the brothers feared Joseph?

3. What was Joseph's reaction to the message from his brothers? (Gen. 50:17b-21)

Joseph called them into his presence and they threw themselves down before him. Offering to make themselves slaves, their posture was a gesture of fear and a request for forgiveness.

4. What were Joseph's words to his brothers who were prostrate before him? (Genesis 50:19-21)

5. Had Joseph really forgiven his brothers? How do you know?

Joseph's example of forgiveness was amazing. The brothers hated him so much they wanted to kill him. They sold him into slavery and yet Joseph realized that in spite of all their hatred and evil deeds that God was in control. God never left him even in the pit or in prison. It had been God's plan to put him into a place of authority and to bring his family into this strange land.

Joseph didn't understand what God's plan was for his life until after God had placed him in the position of vizier of Egypt. He verbalized this message in Genesis 45 as he revealed himself to his brothers. The vision of God's plan for Joseph's life was now clear.

Like Joseph, God does not reveal His ultimate plan for our life at the beginning. He will give us opportunities to serve Him and opportunities of training for a task or purpose He has designed. Whether or not we know the direction our life will take, we are required by God to trust that He knows best in every situation. What seem to us to be tragic events in life may be situations where we are closest to God and the most willing to be obedient. Joseph's situation was not desirable by our standards but God used it nonetheless to train Joseph for an important position that would indeed save the lives of many people and bring his family to a land where they would be isolated and grow into a great nation.

Joseph forgave the injustices that the brothers had done to him because he recognized his role in God's design for his people and in fulfilling the covenant promises God had given to Abraham. How then could he not forgive if he believed God was using him for His purpose?

There are many moments in our own life where we recognize the need to forgive or be forgiven. Like Joseph, if God uses situations in our life to serve His purpose, how can we hold onto unforgiveness?

6. Have you ever had to ask someone to forgive you? What was their reaction? Were you forgiven?

7. Have you ever been convicted to forgive someone for something they did to you? What was your reaction? Were you able to forgive?

8. Are you holding onto unforgiveness for something that has happened to you whether it was an intentional act by someone or not?

While sin doesn't have to be an extravagant event like selling someone into slavery, sin also covers many acts including lying, gossip, hatred, bitterness, etc. We are sinners because we were born with a sin nature. We are unholy and cannot save ourselves.

That is why, God sent His one and only Son into the world to save us from sin:

Romans 5:8 "while we were still sinners, Christ died for us."

Ephesians 1:7 "In him we have redemption through his blood, the forgiveness of sins, in accordance with the riches of God's grace"

1 John 1:9 "If we confess our sins, he is faithful and just to forgive us our sins, and to cleanse us from all unrighteousness."

Jesus is the one who cast our sins as far as the east is from the west. (Psalm 103:12)

As Christians we are saved by the blood of Jesus and we are commanded to forgive others for sins they have committed against us clearly stated in the following passage:

Matthew 6:14-15 "For if you forgive other people when they sin against you, your heavenly Father will also forgive you. But if you do not forgive others their sins, your Father will not forgive your sins."

Knowing that forgiveness comes from Jesus Christ, examine yourself and determine whether you have accepted Jesus as your Lord and Savior. See page 73 for more information on salvation through Jesus Christ and how to become a Christian.

Joseph had many different opportunities for experiencing life. Whether it was in the pit, in Potiphar's house, in prison or in the palace, Joseph was a wise man to use those opportunities God had placed in his path to learn valuable lessons. He was teachable in the bad times and the good times. He was open to God's leading and even when the situation was desperate, Joseph managed to rise above it. Because of this, he was blessed and those around him were also blessed.

9. List some of the life lessons you think Joseph may have learned from his many experiences throughout his life.

We too have been given many experiences and opportunities for learning from the things that God has put in our path. These opportunities to grow your faith and knowledge in Jesus Christ will come until the day you die. How you handle these experiences is up to you. Will you look for the lessons that God has for you or will you wallow in self-pity and miss it? There may be something God is teaching you through this experience or it may simply be an opportunity to show your faith to others. The way you react can be a blessing to those around you.

At this point in your life, you have already had the opportunity to learn many valuable life lessons. Sharing these experiences with others gives encouragement to those going through similar situations. Please share some or these experiences here:

10. What are some of the life lessons you have experienced?

When Joseph died at 110, his body was embalmed in the Egyptian custom. Before his death, Joseph, who believed the promises of God, made his people swear an oath to carry his body out of Egypt when the sons of Jacob left Egypt and returned to the Promised Land.

The children of Jacob would live in Goshen in Egypt and grow into the large nation of Israel. Soon there would be pharaohs who did not know Joseph, and his people would become slaves, mistreated by the Egyptians until the exodus four hundred years later just as God had promised in Genesis 15:13. Led by Moses, the Israelites left Egypt with Joseph's mummified body and returned to the Promised Land.

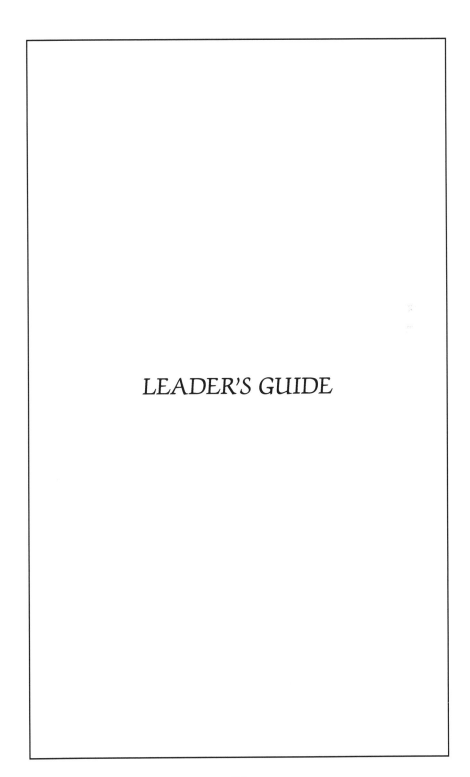

LEADER'S GUIDE

Ancestors

Abraham

1. The acceptable custom of the time allowed the primary wife to give her handmaiden in her place if the primary wife could not conceive children. Sarah decided to help God because it seemed like God was not going to provide a child by her because she was passed childbearing age.

2. Hagar despised Sarah and looked down on her mistress.

3. Before Ishmael was born, Sarah accused Abraham of being responsible for the attitude Hagar had toward her and for Sarah's misery. After Isaac's birth, Ishmael mocked Isaac and Sarah demanded that Hagar and Ishmael be sent away.

4. Sarah mistreated Hagar so she ran away.

5. The Angel of the Lord appeared to her giving her instructions and prophecies for her son.

6. Abraham was 100 years old and Sarah was 90 years old.

7. Sarah and Abraham sent them away. God appeared to Hagar in the desert and promised to make Ishmael a great nation.

Isaac

1. Esau was Isaac's favorite because he was a hunter and outdoorsman.

2. Jacob was Rebekah's favorite because he was quiet and gentle spirit that stayed home near Rebekah.

3. He didn't put any value on the birthright catering to his immediate needs of the moment.

4. Jacob received the blessing of richness of the land, abundant grain, and new wine and the covenant promise that many people would serve him and nations would bow down to him. He would be master over his brother, and those who blessed him would be blessed and those who cursed him would be cursed.

5. Esau wept bitterly and was very angry vowing to kill Jacob for what he had done.

6. Animosity and perhaps jealousy because of the relationship each had with the other parent. Not much communication took place in this family.

7. Isaac and Rebekah were split in helping each child gain the blessing causing dissention between the two of them. Esau and Jacob were estranged for many years.

Jacob

1. Jacob traveled to Haran in search of a wife from among his mother's people and to escape from his brother Esau.

2. Jacob and Rachel first met at the well where she came to water the sheep.

3. Rachel was a shepherdess.

4. Rebekah and Laban were brother and sister.

5. <u>Leah</u>, whose name means "cow," and <u>Rachel</u>, whose name means "ewe." <u>Leah</u> was the eldest daughter. <u>Leah</u> had delicate eyes, while <u>Rachel</u> was beautiful in form and appearance (Gen. 29:15-17).

6. Jacob agreed to serve his uncle for seven years for Rachel's hand in marriage and the time seemed only a few days because Jacob <u>loved</u> Rachel (Gen. 29:18-19).

7. Jacob did not know that Rachel had been switched for Leah because she was the oldest daughter. Jacob agreed to work an additional seven years for Rachel, although Laban let him marry her after Jacob spent a week with Leah.

8. Jacob <u>loved</u> Rachel more than Leah.

9. Personal reflection and opinion answer.

10. Proverbs 14:29 <u>patience with great understanding</u> for the other person

    Proverbs 20:3 <u>avoid strife and quarreling</u>

    James 1:19-21 <u>be quick to listen</u>, <u>slow to speak</u> and <u>slow to anger</u>, <u>get rid of all moral filth</u> in your own life, <u>be humble</u> to accept God's word

    James 4:11-12 <u>do not slander</u> one another, do not speak against anyone or judge them (who are you to judge)

    Ecclesiastes 7:9 <u>do not be quickly provoked or angry</u>

    Ephesians 4:31-32 <u>get rid of all bitterness, rage and anger</u> toward someone, get rid of brawling/fighting, malice and slander; <u>be kind and compassionate, forgiving</u> as Christ forgave you

Romans 12:9-13 <u>have sincere love, hate evil, cling to good, be devoted in love to each other, honor the other person above yourself, seek and serve the Lord, be joyful in hope, patient in affliction, faithful in prayer, share with others in need</u>

1 Peter 1:22-23 <u>obey the truth, love from the heart</u> because you are born again through the living and enduring word of God

1 John 3:18-20 <u>don't just love with words or speech but actions and truth</u>

11. Practice these things: patience and understanding, avoid strife and quarreling, be quick to listen, slow to speak and slow to anger, rid yourself of immorality, do not slander or speak against anyone, get rid of bitterness, rage and anger, be kind and compassionate, forgiving, show love, be faithful in prayer, obey the truth, and love with actions and truth. Jacob did not set a godly example for his family. Had there been more love for everyone, more seeking God, this family may have become more kind and compassionate to each other. All of the above truths teach us how to behave and treat each other with love and respect.

Family Traits

1. Abraham: Believed in God and His promises, a man of faith, friend of God; Sarah: Believed in God; Isaac: Believed in God and His promises; Rebekah: Believed in God's promises that her older son would serve the younger son; Jacob: Believed in God and the covenant promises

2. Abraham: deceived Pharaoh and Abimelech concerning Sarah, participated in the scheme for the promised child; Sarah: schemed to help God fulfill His promise of a child; Isaac: showed favoritism between his sons; Rebekah: helped Jacob fulfill God's promise by deceiving Isaac; Jacob: deceived his father and stole the blessing from his brother

3. Strong faith in God and belief in His promises.

4. Deceitfulness, scheming, "helping" God out, lying to meet the need.

5. Ezekiel states at the end of verse 17, "He will not die for his father's sin; he will surely live." Sins of the father are not the sins of the son. Everyone is accountable for personal sin.

6. Personal answers may vary.

7. Personal answers may vary.

8. "Don't be deceived; the one who leads a life to please his sin nature will reap destruction. The one who leads a life to please God will reap eternal life."

9. This verse reveals that each person is responsible for his or her own sin and those who deceive others will reap the consequences of these actions. Be careful to lead a life pleasing to God. Other opinion answers may vary.

Joseph's Family Life

1. Leah's sons: Reuben, Simeon, Levi, Judah, Issachar, Zebulun; Rachel's sons: Joseph, Benjamin; Bilhah's sons: Dan, Naphtali; Zilpah's sons: Gad, Asher

2. Rachel: Joseph: "God has taken away my disgrace" finally she gave birth and was no longer disgraced among women, Ben-oni: son of her sorrow because she was about to die, Dan: "God has vindicated me" because he was the 1st child that was considered her own, Naptali: the 2nd child of Bilhah "my struggle" because Rachel still wanted a child of her own and this seemed to be the only way she could be justified

   Leah: Reuben: "see a son" to draw attention that she had produced a son, Simeon: "hearing or one who hears" surely Jacob would notice her now, Levi: "attached" now Jacob would have to be attached to her; Judah: "I will praise the Lord" she recognized that she too has a relationship with God, Issachar: "reward" this child is her reward, Zebulun: "honor" Jacob finally treats me with honor, Leah's children by Zilpah were Gad: "good fortune" I am favored because of my children and Asher: "women will call me happy" because I have so many sons.

3. Possession of the birthright meant an inheritance of a double portion of land and family possessions, leadership of the family, being the religious head of the family, and inheriting the covenant promise.

4. Reuben was Jacob's firstborn son, and he lost the birthright because he slept with Jacob's concubine Bilhah.

5. They were passed over for engaging in violence and murder in revenge for the rape of their sister Dinah.

6. Dictionary definitions may vary slightly.

7. Joseph was the son of his old age and the son of the wife he loved most.

8. Jacob openly showed that he loved Joseph more. Joseph was constantly telling on them to their father and provoked anger among his brothers. The birthright might go to Joseph as the first born of Rachel.

9. It represented favoritism and possibly Jacob's intention to give Joseph the birthright.

10. As a teenage boy, he may have felt extra special and perhaps a little better than his brothers.

11. Opinion Answers may vary.

12. Opinion Answers may vary.

13. Jacob could have treated his sons fairly by not showing any favoritism.

14. Fathers, do not provoke your children to anger, lest they be discouraged

15. It helps explain the feelings and actions of the people involved and also gives us an example for examining our own life and actions.

Joseph's Dreams

1. "For God may speak in one way, or in another, yet man does not perceive it. In a dream, in a vision of the night when deep sleep falls upon men, while slumbering on their beds, then He opens the ears of men and seals their instruction".

2. God speaks to men as He chooses through dreams, visions, and other ways. Today God speaks through His Holy Word, through sermons, devotions, songs and any way He desires.

3. Abimelech (Genesis 20:3): God told him in a dream that Sarah was married.

    Jacob (Genesis 28:12, Genesis 31:10-13): First Jacob dreamed of a ladder going to heaven with angels ascending and descending it. In the second dream, God told Jacob to return to the land of his birth.

    Daniel (Daniel 2:19, 7:1): Daniel received God's interpretation of Nebuchadnezzar's dreams, then God gave Daniel night dreams and visions, and the interpretations of these dreams.

    Joseph (Matthew 1:20-21, 2:13): God told Joseph to take Mary as his wife because her child was conceived by the Holy Spirit, and Joseph was told to take Mary and Jesus to Egypt and remain there until he was instructed to return home.

    Paul (Acts 23:11): The Lord told Paul he must witness in Rome.

4. Perhaps Joseph was like some teenage boys, a little bit too sure of himself as well as boastful or prideful.

5. His brother's sheaves would bow down to his sheaves, and Joseph's brothers would one day bow to him.

6. The sun, moon, and eleven stars bowed down to Joseph. One day his whole family would bow before him.

7. The dreams indicated that Joseph would be in a superior position, and his brothers would have to bow before him. Their jealousy would grow stronger and would soon erupt into bitterness with a bent for revenge.

8. Since Jacob had dreams of his own, he respected what dreams meant. He pondered the meaning of Joseph's dreams. No doubt when the brothers brought the coat sprinkled with blood, Jacob thought Joseph was dead. But later, when he saw Joseph alive, he remembered the dreams.

9. Joseph's dreams were prophetic. They gave Joseph a vision of what was to come, and he knew God was with him even though he wasn't sure how God would take him from the pit to a position of authority. It also was a reminder to Joseph's father and brothers after he was vizier of Egypt that God is in control of every life and all things.

10. Dictionary definitions may vary slightly.

11. Many of the words in this definition describe the ways the brothers were feeling or acting.

12. Dictionary definitions may vary slightly but many of the words used in the definition fit with the attitudes the brothers experienced.

13. These two words are very closely related as one leads into the other. First feelings of jealousy are felt and as they intensify, bitterness begins to set in.

14. Personal reflection answer.

15. Personal reflection answer.

16. Personal reflection answer.

17. Opinions may vary.

18. Dictionary definitions may vary slightly.

19. "And his brothers saw that their father loved him more than all his brothers; and so they <u>hated</u> him and <u>could not speak to him on friendly terms</u> . . . then Joseph had a dream, and when he told it to his brothers, they <u>hated him even more</u> . . . so they <u>hated</u> him even more for his dreams and for his words . . . and his brothers were <u>jealous</u> of him, but his father kept the saying in mind" (Genesis 37:4-5,8,11 NIV).

20. The best response is to repent of your bitterness, anger, jealousy, and hatred, and confess it to God, who saves you from your sin.

21. Ephesians 4:31-32: "<u>Get rid of all bitterness, rage and anger, brawling and slander, along with every form of malice. Be kind and compassionate</u> to one another, <u>forgiving</u> each other, just as in Christ God forgave you".

    Hebrews 12:15: "<u>See to it that</u> <u>no one misses the grace of God</u> and that <u>no bitter root</u> grows up to cause trouble and defile many".

    Romans 13:13-14: "Let us <u>behave decently</u>, as in the daytime, not in orgies and drunkenness, not in sexual immorality and debauchery, not in dissension and jealousy. Rather, <u>clothe yourselves with the Lord Jesus Christ</u>, and do not think about how to gratify the desires of the sinful nature".

    James 3:14: "But if you have bitter jealousy and selfish ambition in your heart, <u>do not be arrogant and so lie against the truth</u>".

Sold into Slavery

1. Opinions may vary. Possible answers-Joseph might have been surprised by the actions of his brothers and their attitudes. He was afraid of their talk of murder, sorrowful for his father, and dread of what lay ahead.

2. Reuben would have to answer to Jacob as to why Reuben let Joseph die. He didn't want to be responsible for his death. He planned to come back and rescue Joseph from the pit and take him home.

3. He chose to have someone else take care of Joseph so that if he died, his blood would be on someone else's hands. He saw it as a perfect solution to the problem.

4. Twenty shekels of silver.

5. Beyond despair, possibly anger for what was happening, hurt to the core.

6. Reuben tore his clothes as a sign of mourning and said to his brothers, the boy is not there! Where can I turn now!

7. Ripped Joseph's coat to shreds, soaked it in goat's blood to show Jacob evidence of what happened.

8. They told Jacob an animal had eaten Joseph.

9. Jacob tore his clothes, put on sackcloth, mourned for many days, and refused to be comforted.

Potiphar's House

1. Joseph's family lived in tents with household items that could be rolled up and carried easily as they moved. Beds were mostly fabric place on the ground. When Joseph went to Egypt this urban society where he lived had mud brick homes, furniture, beds with wooden carvings, every thing the "modern" society had to offer.

2. Opinions may vary. Served food and drink, cleaned household, tended to the garden, ran errands, and anything he was told to do.

3. He was willing to serve to the best of his ability, responsible and respectful and Potiphar took note.

4. Psalm 37:7: "Be still before the Lord and wait patiently for him; do not fret when men succeed in their ways, when they carry out their wicked schemes".

   Proverbs 15:13: "A happy heart makes the face cheerful, but heartache rushes the spirit".

5. Have a cheerful heart, wait patiently, and do not fret or worry.

6. The Lord was with him.

7. Personal reflection answer.

8. Personal reflection answer.

9. Have a humble attitude, be content and trust that God will take care of you.

10. He refused her advances and asked how he could do such a wicked thing and sin against God.

11. Joseph was prepared to act according to what he knew pleased God. Scripture says to watch and pray so that you will not fall into temptation.

12. He did not allow temptation to overcome him. He gave a verbal acknowledgement of God.

13. Joseph quickly left the place where she was. He was fleeing from temptation. Scripture tells us that God is faithful and will not let you be tempted beyond what you can bear. He will also provide a way out so that you can stand up under temptation.

14. Potiphar may have had doubts about what actually happened but he had to act on behalf of his wife. Opinion answers may vary.

15. Opinion answers may vary. Possibly Potiphar didn't completely believe his wife or he had such great respect for Joseph he didn't think execution was justified.

16. Opinion answers vary. He probably thought he didn't have a choice. He had to appease an angry woman!

17. Personal refection answer.

Joseph in Prison

1. Philippians 4:11-13: "I am not saying this because I am in need, for I have learned to be content whatever the circumstances. I know what it is to be in need, and I know what it is to have plenty. I have learned the secret of being content in any and every situation, whether well fed or hungry, whether living in plenty or in want. I can do everything through him who gives me strength".

   1 Thessalonians 5:18: "Pray continually; give thanks in all circumstances, for this is God's will for you in Christ Jesus".

2. He learned to be content in whatever the circumstances because he knew that it was through God that he could be strong. Joseph prayed often, thanking the Lord for all his blessings.

3. The warden, who put Joseph in charge of the other prisoners.

4. Joseph's had the ability to lead and take care of the duties that were assigned to him, just as he did while serving in Potiphar's house. He was compassionate and caring for others. He was a quick learner and quickly picked up knowledge of new things.

5. At the appropriate time, the cupbearer would remember the interpretation of his dream, what had happened to the baker and he would tell Pharaoh about it.

6. Personal reflection answer.

7. He was disappointed, patient and continued with his daily tasks.

8. Person reflection answer.

9. Proper court etiquette and inner workings of Pharaoh's court, Egyptian law. The Egyptian language-written and speaking, customs and etiquette of Egyptian society, etc.

10. Accounting, administration, ability to lead, ability to carry out assigned tasks, language and speaking skills, the ability to work well with others, knowledge of law and the inner workings of Pharaoh's court and military.

Pharaoh's Dream

1. The magicians and wise men of Egypt

2. They were supposed to be the wisest and most knowledgeable men in Egypt.

3. Dreams were given by the gods and held special meaning about the future.

4. The chief cupbearer remembered that Joseph had interpreted his dream and the chief baker's dream, and the results were true.

5. He did not want to offend Pharaoh with his uncleanliness. Egyptians were very conscience of personal hygiene.

6. There would be seven years of plentiful harvest and seven years of famine.

7. Joseph told Pharaoh to put a discerning and wise man in charge, appoint commissioners over the land to take a fifth of the harvest during the seven years of abundance, and collect all the food during these good years, store up the grain, and keep it in the cities to be held in reserve and used during the seven years of famine.

8. He was pleased. He put Joseph in charge of his palace, and all the people of Egypt were to submit to Joseph's orders. Only Pharaoh would be greater than Joseph.

9. His signet ring, robes of fine linen, a gold chain, and a wife named Asenath.

10. Zaphenath-paneah

11. Thirty years old

12. "Thus far the Lord has helped us."

13. While the Ebenezer stone came much later in the history of the Hebrew nation, it was a symbol to the Israelites of God's divine care, provision and protection. Joseph understood the covenant promises of God. God had helped Joseph up to this point in his life and Joseph was confident that God would continue to help him and bring about His divine purposes and plan for His people until the day he died.

14. We should also remember how God has brought us through times of trials and struggles in our life and guided and protected us. If He has taken care of us in the past, and to this point, He certainly will do so for the rest of our lives.

Fat and the Famine

1. Joseph prayed for guidance and wisdom in fulfilling his responsibilities. He surveyed the land, learned where all the crops were raised, located existing storage facilities and possible sites for new ones, determine existing ways for accounting grain and developed new plans for accounting abundance, and more.

2. Proverbs 16:3 "Commit to the Lord whatever you do, and he will establish your plans."

   Proverb 19:21 "Many are the plans in a person's heart, but it is the Lord's purpose that prevails."

   Isaiah 23:9: "The Lord Almighty planned it, to bring low the pride of all glory and to humble all who are renowned on the earth".

   Isaiah 30:1: "'Woe to the obstinate children,' declares the Lord, 'to those who carry out plans that are not mine, forming an alliance, but not by my Spirit, heaping sin upon sin'".

3. We are to commit all of our plans to the Lord, God's plan will prevail, we should not rely on anything but God's help, He alone is Almighty

4. Personal reflection answer.

5. Joseph was blessed from God with two sons: Manasseh and Ephraim.

6. Joseph opened the storehouses and sold grain to the Egyptians and people from other countries because the famine was severe everywhere.

7. The money he collected from Egypt and Canaan were given to Pharaoh.

8. When the people ran out of money, Joseph took livestock in trade for grain.

9. When all the livestock belonged to Pharaoh, the people sold themselves as slaves.

10. The seeds were given to plant on the land that now belonged to Pharaoh. They were to plant and harvest the crops and give one-fifth of it to Pharaoh keeping four-fifths for themselves.

Joseph and His Brothers

1. He immediately recognized them and remembered his dreams from his youth.

2. He spoke harshly to them and accused them of being spies because he wanted to test their motives.

3. The brothers told Joseph they were the sons of one man. They were honest men. There were twelve brothers, the youngest was at home and one was no more.

4. He wanted to know for sure they had changed and were not filled with hatred as they had been.

5. Sitting in prison, the brothers would have a chance to reflect on past deeds and reasons they were in their current situation.

6. They started to argue and thought they were being punished for what they had done to Joseph.

7. Guilt does not have a time schedule. Sometimes it lasts a lifetime. They may have thought finally after all this time they were receiving what they deserved.

8. They all felt guilty for what they had done to Joseph, but it was easier to blame someone else than accept responsibility.

9. He turned away from them and began to weep. Joseph probably had many emotions: grief, sorrow, longing for restitution.

10. Simeon was the oldest brother after Reuben left the day the brothers had planned to kill Joseph. Also, perhaps Joseph wanted to test Simeon a little further.

11. He did this to see what his brothers would do. It was to test them.

12. He assumed Simeon was lost forever because Jacob would never let Benjamin go back to Egypt. This saddened him greatly.

13. He knew they could not return to Egypt to buy grain unless Benjamin accompanied them.

14. Perhaps Reuben was not trust worthy based on previous actions. He could not trust his precious Benjamin to leave his sight with Reuben in charge.

15. 1 Corinthians 13:1-3: "If I speak in the tongues of men and of angels, but have not love, I am only a resounding gong or a clanging cymbal. If I have the gift of prophecy and can fathom all mysteries and all knowledge, and if I have a faith that can move mountains, but have not love, I am nothing. If I give all I possess to the poor and surrender my body to the flames, but have not love, I gain nothing".

    Matthew 7:15-20: "Watch out for false prophets. They come to you in sheep's clothing, but inwardly they are ferocious wolves. By their fruit you will recognize them. Do people pick grapes from thorn bushes, or figs from thistles? Likewise every good tree bears good fruit, but a bad tree bears bad fruit. A good tree cannot bear bad fruit, and a bad tree cannot bear good fruit. Every tree that does not bear good fruit is cut down and thrown into the fire. Thus, by their fruit you will recognize them."

    Proverbs 15:14: "The discerning heart seeks knowledge, but the mouth of a fool feeds on folly."

The discerning heart can determine the truth by watching the actions of those that proclaim their heart is true.

Return to Egypt

1. Jacob's family had eaten all the grain they had brought from Egypt, and the famine had not yet subsided.

2. Jacob realized the severity of the situation, and that the family needed grain or everyone would die. He didn't have a choice.

3. They took the best products of the land: balm, honey, spices, myrrh, pistachios and almonds, and double the amount of silver found in their sacks.

4. They were invited to dinner at Joseph's house and treated kindly.

5. They thought they were being brought to Joseph's home because of the silver that was found in their sacks the first time. They feared they would be attacked, overpowered, and seized as slaves and their donkeys would be taken away.

6. "Don't be afraid, the God of your father has given you treasure in your sacks; I received your silver."

7. He hurried into a private room and wept. He then washed his face, came out and, controlling himself, told the servants to serve the food.

8. The brothers were seated in order of their ages, from the firstborn to the youngest.

9. It was detestable to the Egyptians because they prided themselves on being clean. The Hebrews' main occupation of raising sheep was considered an unclean job.

10. Joseph was testing to see whether the other brothers showed any jealousy or animosity toward Benjamin.

The Final Test

1. A servant, carrying out Joseph's instructions, put Joseph's silver cup in Benjamin's grain sack to see how the brothers would react when the cup was found and Benjamin would be in trouble for it.

2. When the servant accused them of stealing, the brothers were so certain the servant was wrong, they swore death to the one in whose sack it was found and slavery to the rest. Joseph's servant found the silver cup placed in Benjamin sack and the brothers were horrified as they return to Egypt.

3. The man who was found to have the cup would become a slave or could have been executed.

4. Judah was concerned that his father would die if Benjamin did not return. Judah offered to remain in Benjamin's place.

5. He saw they were more concerned about their father than their own well being and what would happen to Jacob if Benjamin did not return. Had they been the same old brothers, they would have left Benjamin in Egypt to get rid of him.

6. Joseph sent the servants from the room and he was so overcome with emotions he wept and wailed. He revealed his identity.

7. Is my father still living?

8. He told them not to be distressed or angry with themselves. God had sent him down to Egypt not them. God had sent him ahead to save many lives.

9. Four times; Joseph was acknowledging that it was God's plan that had brought him to Egypt and God's plan that was still working. Joseph had a personal relationship with God

10. Pharaoh was pleased and gave instructions for Joseph to bring his father and the rest of the family members to Egypt. Pharaoh would give them the best of the land of Egypt to enjoy.

11. Joseph gave them carts, provisions for the journey, new clothing to each with Benjamin receiving five sets of clothes and 300 shekels of silver, 10 donkeys loaded with the best things of Egypt, and 10 female donkeys loaded with grain, bread and other provisions.

12. "Do not quarrel on the way!" He knew the brothers quarreled often.

A Family Reunion

1. Jacob thought Joseph was dead so he did not believe them until they told him everything Joseph had said to them and saw the carts Joseph had sent to carry him back.

2. He went to Beersheba to offer thanksgiving sacrifices to God for the life of his son Joseph and to receive direction from God concerning the move to Egypt. Jacob had learned to rely on God and His will.

3. Don't be afraid to go to Egypt. God would make a great nation of Jacob's descendents and God would be with them and bring them back again.

4. Joseph would be there with Jacob to care for him until the day he died.

5. 66 people coming down to Egypt with Jacob not counting the wives plus Joseph and his two sons and Jacob were seventy in all.

6. Accurate record keeping was important especially in this case to show how this group of God's chosen people would grow to be a very large nation. It gives an idea how fast they grew in four hundred years when this number is subtracted from the number leaving in the exodus.

7. They embraced and wept for a long time.

8. Jacob told Joseph he was ready to die since he was able to see that Joseph was still alive.

9. It was the best part of Egypt and provided the sons of Jacob rich pasture land and water for raising crops and herds.

10. Because they were shepherds, they were not included in social activities or associations with Egyptians. Shepherds were considered dirty and unclean and were detested by the Egyptian culture. Because of this, Jacob's people would be separated and most likely not intermarry with Egyptians and would grow into a purer Hebrew nation away from the pagan culture of many gods. God would protect them from the famine, from other cultures that would sway them away from Him and would grow them into a large nation as He planned.

11. Seventeen years.

Blessings and Burial

1. The right hand was thought to be the one through which spiritual blessings were given and represented strength and favor. The son who had the right hand placed upon his head received the greater blessing. It was a common practice to bless the older son over the younger son.

2. Jacob adopted Joseph's sons as his own giving them an inheritance equal to his other sons and blessed them. He then gave Joseph the ridge of land he gained by defeating the Amorites.

3. Simeon and Levi

4. They had murdered in a great slaughter the men of Shecham because of the rape of their sister Dinah.

5. Joseph

6. Reuben slept with Bilhah, Jacob's wife.

7. Judah's blessings would include a dynasty of kings that would remain in the house of Judah until Shiloh (Messiah) comes.

8. In the cave in the field of Machpelah, near Mamre, in Canaan, which Abraham bought as a burial place from Ephron the Hittite.

9. Abraham, Isaac, Rebekah, and Leah

10. Opinion answer. Most likely because he trusted Joseph more than the others.

11. 130, 17, 147

12. He threw himself upon Jacob kissed him and wept.

13. He was embalmed per Egyptian custom. To have traveled back to Canaan without the body being embalmed would not have been appropriate due to the heat of the desert.

14. All of Pharaoh's officials, dignitaries of Egypt including Pharaoh's court, all of the members of Joseph's household, and all that belonged to Jacob's household accompanied Joseph as they returned to Canaan. Only the children and their flocks and herds were left in Goshen.

15. At the threshing floor of Atad, Joseph observed a seven-day period of mourning for his father. Other reasons for stopping there might have included feeding the large number of animals that accompanied them and to offer sacrifices to God before they crossed the Jordan.

Forgiveness

1. Opinion answers may vary.

2. The brothers were unsure whether Joseph had truly forgiven them. Thinking he tolerated them because of their father, they were afraid for their lives. Guilt had consumed them.

3. Joseph wept and then he reassured them and spoke kindly to them.

4. "Don't be afraid. Am I in the place of God? You intended to harm me, but God intended it for good to accomplish what is now being done, the saving of many lives."

5. Yes, through his actions.

6. Personal reflection answer.

7. Personal reflection answer.

8. Personal reflection answer.

9. To be content in every situation, work to the best of your ability no matter where you are, treat all people with compassion, God is in control of all things and His plan will be done, all things work together for good according to His purpose, use the gifts the Lord gives you in His service, adversity creates opportunities to grow your faith, forgive as God has forgiven you. And other opinion answers.

10. Personal reflection answer.

JOSEPH'S STORY

Jacob and Rachel's firstborn son
Wore a coat of colors, this favored one.
Jealousy, bitterness, and hatred too
Were shown by his brothers; oh what would they do?

One day in a pasture, he was thrown in a pit.
Joseph cried and he pleaded, but in spite of the fit,
He was sold to the Midianites for shekels twenty.
The brothers were pleased and thought they had plenty.

Sold by his brothers to become a young slave,
His father would mourn and threaten the grave.
Though the brothers meant evil, God turned it for good
To save many lives God knew that He would.

To Egypt he traveled in a vast caravan;
Bound in strong chains, he belonged to the man.
His life changed forever; this young boy would be
A slave to Egyptians not to roam free.

A slave, a servant, and a prisoner too:
Joseph often thought that his life might be through.
But he learned that he must be willing to stand
And follow the leading of God's special plan.

The gift that God gave him as a revealer of dreams,
Preparing him to overcome the author of schemes.
His dreams of power would certainly come true,
But in God's perfect timing as only God can do.

From Potiphar's house to prison to court,
In time he'd be placed o'er each field and each port.
In charge of the land and sea was his job,
Storing abundance the coming famine would rob.

God blessed him with riches and even a wife
To bring Joseph joy from past sadness and strife.
He had sons to his name and great power as well,
With respect from each person o'er valley and dell.

Large numbers did travel to Egypt each day
To purchase some grain for which they would pay.
This vizier of Pharaoh, hear them he must
And determine their plight from daylight to dusk.

Then one day he saw them, his brothers of ten
Come to Egypt to buy food and request it of him.
A sadness was felt deep down in his heart,
And he knew he must be careful and cunning and smart.

They humbly bowed down before his presence that day,
Not knowing this man was the one they betrayed.
Joseph questioned their hearts and their motives as well.
He accused them of spying and sent them to jail.

After three days, only Simeon would stay
In the prison locked up awaiting that day
When the brothers brought Benjamin for Joseph to see.
Would he believe their innocence and would they go free?

The brothers appeared with Benjamin in tow.
To Joseph's for dinner they'd sit in a row,
From oldest to youngest. What a surprise:
A great abundance of food before their eyes.

Was the jealousy, bitterness, or hatred still there?
Were their hearts full of guilt and did they now care
For Jacob and Benjamin and what they had done
To Jacob and Rachel's once favored son?

To prove their remorse, Joseph devised a shrewd test:
A silver cup found in the sack, which Benjamin possessed.
Would the brothers stand by him or leave him behind?
Did they still hold that hatred or would they be kind?

The brothers returned to Joseph's grand place
To plead for the brother that caused this disgrace.
Judah fell on his face before this powerful man
And begged for Benjamin's life, that was his plan.

Joseph saw in their hearts their distress and concern
For Jacob and Benjamin and so he discerned
The brothers had repented of their terrible sin,
So he revealed who he was and wept once again.

Terror filled the hearts of the brothers that day,
For they knew not what Joseph might do or say.
Forgiveness he offered and forgiveness he gave,
Like Jesus who died that you might be saved.

Remember when someone sins against you,
Take care that you offer forgiveness too.
You never know where the Lord's plan will lead.
It may be that you also have thousands to feed!

ABOUT THE AUTHOR

Sandra Hardage

Sandra Hardage defines her life with the gifts and blessings God has given her. Her faith in Christ as Savior and her family, including her husband, children, and grandchildren, are the chief blessings in her life.

From the age of ten, God began to stir a desire in her heart to become a teacher. Because of this desire, Sandra has been involved with education all her life. She has taught in public school in all grades but third and sixth, taught as an adjunct college professor, and was coordinator of a (televised) GED-ONTV program, an adult education learning center and coordinator of the technology, distance learning and media programs for an education cooperative serving twenty-seven school districts. Sandra has been a Sunday school teacher and Bible study leader; as well as an associational women's ministry director. She is currently teaching an online Bible study.

Sandra holds BSE and MSE degrees and has taken many courses to hone the skills needed for the jobs God gave her, including classes in computers, curriculum, computer networking, Web design, distance learning, and new technologies.

She feels that every area of teaching and learning were preparation for her current role as creator and founder of the online ministry My Journey of Faith. Sandra hopes God will use this ministry to encourage Christians and uplift the name of Jesus Christ.

My Journey of Faith ministry's website is a gathering place for encouraging Christians in their daily journey of life and includes blogs, My Journey of Faith Online Magazine, My Journey of Faith BlogTalk radio, Bible studies, inspirational photography, My Journey of Faith Book Club on Facebook and more.

There are many who share their life experiences to encourage others on our journey with Christ. Join Sandra and others at the ministry website http://myjourneyoffaith.com and My Journey of Faith Facebook Page. Find Sandra's author page at http://SandraHardage.com